Sex, Marriage, Gays & God

Pastor Thomas Gross

xulon PRESS

Bible quotations are taken from :

The Vine's Expository Dictionary of Old Testament Words. Copyright © 1985 by Thomas Nelson Publishers; The Vine's Expository Dictionary of Biblical Words. Copyright © 1985 by Thomas Nelson Publishers; The Webster's Random House Dictionary. Copyright © 1999 by Random House Inc.; The Keil & Delitzsch Commentary on the Old Testament: New Updated Edition, Electronic Database. Copyright © 1996 by Hendrickson Publishers, Inc.; The ILLUSTRATED BIBLE DICTIONARY, M. G. EASTON, Third Edition. Published by Harper & Brothers, 1903, PC Study Bible formatted electronic

Some bible verses will have underlined words or phrases followed by a bracketed or parenthetical word or phrase. The underlined, bracketed, or parenthetical words or phrases in the bible text are the author's insertion designed for clarity and are denoted by an asterisk (*) after the chapter and verse citation. All verses that do not specify a bible version are from the King James Version.

www.xulonpress.com

PREFACE

*T*he reason for writing this book was born out my sensing the need to teach the church I pastor regarding this very controversial topic of gay marriage and about the relevant issues that are being raised about homosexuality on a continual basis. As a result, I had begun a teaching series on the topic from a biblical perspective. But I soon discovered that this was a much bigger subject than it initially appeared to be, mainly because I had discovered that one cannot simply say that homosexuality is wrong, and then expect that everything will be understood by those who oppose that position. People are much more complicated than that, and the people who advocate the gay lifestyle attempt to use scripture to justify their positions and have raised many questions that are not always being answered satisfactorily by some in the church.

I also discovered that I was not going to do justice to this topic during my series, even though I had intended to cover it for several weeks.

As it turned out, not everyone was present for all of the series which was not good for the continuity of understanding, and even so, I knew that there were many more people across America and the world that really needed or perhaps even wanted to hear these things that would not be present either. Additionally, some information that is very sensitive needed to be presented and in some cases, the forum of the church was not always appropriate for some of the more explicit subject matter if very young children were present. Then, because of time constraints, a lot of information would be omitted. After about three weeks or so into the series, I realized this subject would be better served if put into a book, and that I would eventually do that at some time in the future.

After hearing of the constant controversies about gay marriage rights, the issuances of gay marriage licenses, lawsuits in favor of gay marriage rights and licenses, activist judge orders, and court cases regarding gay marriage and civil contracts, I was prompted to begin this writing. The purpose of this book is to enlighten all who read and give the bases for the traditional biblical postulations of homosexuality and male-female marriage.

My approach to this work is one of honesty about the things that are controversial that ordinarily raise questions in which the answers are uncomfortable, not well understood, or avoided by church people who are in turn accused of "picking and choosing" what they want to believe from the bible about homosexuality. And truthfully, some church people do not always understand the things that are written in the bible, especially the Old Testament, and they tend to erroneously write them off as unnecessary and unneeded because they believe that in these days, God is "doing something new." But I have learned that one cannot fully understand the things of God without understanding what is written in the Old Testament. The apostle Paul wrote, "For whatsoever things were written aforetime were written for our learning ..." (Romans 15:4) If they are "written for our learning," then what are those things trying to teach us? Therefore, I am not going to evade the scriptures that are uncomfortable. People need to understand how and why the Old Testament is the foundation of the New Testament and how the two testaments correlate.

I have added a personal testimony in which I am not attempting to be sensual or titillating, nor am I trying to say anything shocking. I am only being honest about the things that have affected me, and have silently affected others. It is not easy to write those things about myself, but I want to show what has been repeated over and over in the lives of many others and what is damaging to our families, communities, and nations today. While the information is shameful, it is not new or unique. You won't hear many people discussing it much because it is easier to bury it and not face it again. The goal of presenting my issues is to also present the remedy that God has made available to each of us by showing what God has delivered me from. God can deliver any one of us from anything that disturbs us when we call upon The Name of Jesus for that deliverance.

Some of this will be offensive and make some readers angry. While that is not my intention, offense is not my fault. Offense is the result of something going on within a person that they themselves do not fully understand, and their anger is thus misdirected.

The information within this book is in no way a message of hatred and is not based on any fear of homosexuality on my part nor should it be construed as such. Such conclusions cannot be honestly reached from the reading of this book. Unless the reader reads the entire book, its complete message cannot be properly ascertained. The information within the work is based on the truth of the word of God, the love of God, and His desire for our salvation which is the gift of eternal life.

Foreword

*T*homas Gross has been a pastor for twenty-six years in the denominational district where I currently serve as District Superintendent. He and his wife, Tawanna, have demonstrated their commitment to the call to ministry in many ways. Their resolve to stay in ministry in New Orleans after the horrible destruction of Katrina is just one of the many ways they exemplify being servants of God. Their integrity and humility are easily observed by the way they live.

Thomas has written a direct, no-holds-barred treatise on what are often considered delicate and controversial subjects. His own experiences, subsequent conversion as well as obvious deep studies, give him insight into these areas that many do not have. The illustration of teaching his son how to keep himself pure in an impure world shows that Thomas is not just writing a book of theories, but that he has also developed strategies to face the issues. If more people would develop strategies for addressing these issues within all society strata, particularly that of our youth, many of our moral dilemmas would diminish dramatically. Some of our social problems as well as sexually transmitted diseases would also see a decline.

Thomas has written the true answer to the moral issues of this permissive and promiscuous society: follow God's word. When we do follow God's principles as well as teach others to do so, we will help this society regain its moral compass.

Thank you, Thomas, for putting this work in print. Our world needs the straight talk.

Superintendent Douglas Fulenwider
Louisiana District Assemblies of God

ACKNOWLEDGEMENTS

I want to thank my wife Tawanna and my daughter Tiara for their patience in putting up with me in the long hours that it took for me to prepare for and write this book. I also want to thank my good friend Pastor Teresa Reiger for her work and effort to preserve the first six chapters of this book. I had printed those chapters for her to have a sneak preview and had not made any hard copies for myself, nor did I have a current disk back-up of the manuscript. Right after I had given her that copy, I had a hard drive failure. Before I could get the hard copy back from her to scan back into the computer, hurricane Katrina hit New Orleans and caused everyone to evacuate. No one knew where anyone else was for at least three weeks. It was not until about four or five weeks later that I had finally gotten in touch with Pastor Reiger. She told me that she had taken the manuscript with her just before she evacuated, even while leaving her *own* papers that she was writing for a class assignment. For that, I am deeply indebted and grateful to her for her act of kindness. That prevented me from having to start all over again, repeating the hours and hours of research, reading, and writing. And finally but more importantly, I give thanks to God for the grace to produce this work.

Chapter One

THE MARRIAGE PRECEDENT

The bible reveals to us that God intended for sexual intercourse to be done only between a man and a woman who are married to each other. It was given to us by God to teach us His righteous laws and His will. Apart from the bible, the truth of sexual issues cannot be properly ascertained because it is the medium which God has ordained to transmit His truths and His standard to mankind. While there are different opinions about marriage and who may have the "right" to marry, God had set the marriage precedent when He created Adam and Eve and bonded them into a lifelong covenant. Their marriage was recorded and preserved in the bible so that it would transcend all peoples and cultures of all time.

God set the marriage precedent by going through a symbolic search to make two very important points. The first is that it was not good for the man to be alone, and the second is that Adam would need a companion who would complement him. The fact that man needs and desires companionship is no accident. God created within Adam his desire for companionship, and not just any kind of companionship, but a very special kind of companionship. The symbolic search happened like this: after God created Adam, He immediately created animal life.

And out of the ground the LORD God formed every beast of the field, and every fowl of the air; and brought them unto Adam to see what he would call them: and whatsoever Adam called every living creature, that was the name thereof. Genesis 2:19

The search was made to find an appropriate companion for Adam among the animals. However, among them there was not a suitable mate.

And Adam gave names to all cattle, and to the fowl of the air, and to every beast of the field; but for Adam there was not found an help meet for him. Genesis 2:20

Adam had even named all of the animals, but none of them drew his interest as a companion. Why? Because God made Adam in such a way that only one species of creation would appropriately appeal to his desire, and that species had not yet been created. God did it that way on purpose as a lesson to us.

Adam was all that God intended him to be, having all the desires that God intended for him to have as a man. He was the prototype man and the crown of creation, created in God's own image. He would set the standard of God's will for all time where God's intent for marriage and mating were concerned. The symbolic search also teaches that God never intended for people to mate with animals. Even without knowledge of this written account, we instinctively know that not only are animals unsuitable for mating with humans, but also that humans were not designed to mate with animals, despite the fact that in many cases it may be physically possible. A later chapter will further explain this instinctive knowledge.

The Appropriate Companion

And the LORD God said, It is not good that the man should be alone; I will make him an help meet for him. Genesis 2:18

God made Adam in such a way that caused him to require a very special kind of companion. This companion would be one who was proper for him in God's eyes and who would set a precedent for all of mankind to come. Again, this companion was not only suitable where Adam was concerned, but was also approved where God was concerned.

In order to create a companion especially for Adam, God put Adam to sleep and removed a rib from his torso. Then around that rib, He fashioned another species of human being, wholly similar to Adam, yet completely different from him. When Adam was awakened and saw his companion for the first time, he made a revelatory exclamation saying,

> *...This is now bone of my bones, and flesh of my flesh: she shall be called Woman, because she was taken out of Man. Therefore shall a man leave his father and his mother, and shall cleave unto his wife: and they shall be one flesh.* Genesis 2:23-24

Whenever a man is "in tune" with God, it is because he is aware of what God wants and his desire is to give God what He wants. Adam made the statement that a man, when leaving his father and mother for companionship, should be joined to his wife. The will of God is for a man to have a woman and not a man for a companion. Unfortunately, when people are not "in tune" with God, they are unaware of what God wants and will as a result, jump to erroneous conclusions and do what they themselves want.

The apostle Paul, also expressing the will of God through revelation and the inspiration of the Holy Spirit on this very same issue, wrote:

> *"For the man is not of the woman; but the woman of the man. Neither was the man created for the woman; but the woman for the man.* 1 Corinthians 11: 8-9

So then, according to the nature of things, the woman was created for the man and not vice versa because God wanted to create a companion who was complementary to Adam. In doing so, He established the marriage precedent. The idea that God only wanted a woman to be a man's lifelong mate is difficult to argue against because the alternatives, a male with another male, or a female with another female living as companions were never positively alluded or referred to in scripture, neither was there a precedent set for such relationships directly by God. Thus, the alternatives were never deemed valid nor is there any record of their approval by God. Besides, such a mating was and is contradictory to His plan of reproduction which would have never occurred at all if God would have created a same-sex mate for Adam. When people behave or act otherwise, they deny the obvious and live in defiance against the will of God.

About Divorce

So the very first marriage formed in the Garden of Eden set a precedent. God made a female human mate for a man and then joined that man and that female together in a holy and Fatherly approval of their union by bestowing His blessing upon them, and upon the children who would be the result of that union. Eve's marriage to Adam commenced when God took Adam's rib and formed Eve around it. Now they were one because Eve had a part of Adam inside her and she owed that part of her existence to Adam.

They were joined that way by God in a physical symbolic oneness designed to teach that a husband and wife should not separate. Adam's rib cannot be removed from the woman without damaging and weakening her, and the rib would die outside of the woman signifying that in separation, a part of him dies. By this we can correctly conclude that marriages are, according to the adage, indeed "made in heaven" (or at least on earth by God). No marriage is valid unless it is approved by God and it is He who actually does the uniting, cultural and civil ceremonies notwithstanding, although they are appropriate and necessary according to the legal demands of existing cultures. The necessity of God's validation is what Jesus emphasized to His disciples when another question came up while He was teaching on marriage and divorce in answer to a question posed to Him by his disciples. They had initially asked whether it was alright for divorce to be granted for any reason whatsoever. He answered by saying,

> *"Have you not read that He who made them at the beginning `made them male and female, `and said, `For this reason a man shall leave his father and mother and be joined to his wife, and the two shall become one flesh? So then, they are no longer two but one flesh. <u>Therefore what God has joined together</u> let not man separate."* Matthew *19:4-6* NKJV*

The passage helps us to understand what God wants out of marriage where any couple is concerned. The words "at the beginning" means that a precedent had been set. Following upon that, Jesus demonstrates that God is not at all pleased about the way that numerous couples (even Christians) treat this God-ordained covenant relationship. The dissolving of a marriage is never good, and it is especially evil when that marriage covenant is broken because of a sexual relationship that takes place with someone else! The prophet Malachi chided with men who divorced their wives when they had gotten older, and then replaced them with other women who were idolaters, or those who married other women who were idolaters while ignoring the first wife altogether by saying,

> *"This is another thing you do: you cover the altar of the LORD with tears, with weeping and with groaning, because He no longer regards the offering or accepts it with favor from your hand." Yet you say, `For what reason?' Because the LORD has been a witness between you and the wife of your youth, against whom you have dealt treacherously, though she is your companion and your wife by covenant.* Malachi 2:13-14 NASU

There are some who may attempt to justify gay relationships because of the high divorce rate, and especially because of the high divorce rate taking place within the church. But a wrong is never vindicated by another wrong. What you end up with is some in the church doing wrong as well as those outside the church doing wrong who are also in danger of God's judgment.

Marriage is a product of God, and divorce is a product of man. When divorce happens, something sinful is going on within either the husband, or the wife, or both. Sin is not God's fault, nor was it created by God. The English word *sin* is translated from the Hebrew word *chata* and the Greek word *hamartia*, both of which have the root meaning of *missing a mark or an intended target*. God's "mark" or goal or target is what He wants, and what He wants is His standard of righteousness produced within us. However, when we do what is contrary to His will, we miss God's "target" of righteousness which is His will. The bible calls that "miss" sin. Our very nature is sinful simply because it is self-willed and self-centered from infancy. Not long after birth our nature has us committing self-centered actions like taking another child's toy, hitting another child, defying our parents, or lying about something, knowing full well inside that what we are doing is not right despite being very young and naive. We are born into this world driven by an ego-centric nature that is difficult to control. King David, understanding the root of that nature lamented over it saying,

> *Behold, I was shapen in iniquity; and in sin did my mother conceive me.* Psalms 51:5

Sin is a nature within us, that drives us to do our own thing and ignore God, reasonable logic, wisdom, law, and all that is good, sometimes even to our own destruction. We try hard to understand our flawed nature, but we have difficulty doing so because it is not something we can fully understand without revelation from God. But initially for most of us, God is the *last* someone our human nature wants for guidance and direction because He "cramps our style." The apostle Paul explained it this way:

> "...because the mind set on the flesh is hostile toward God, for it does not subject itself to the law of God, for it is not even able to do so ..." Romans 8:7 NASU

Our human nature driven mind (called "the flesh" in the bible), does not like God or care for the things of God, despite the fact that we know in our minds that anything that God says to us is right.

So initially we run from and avoid God, not wanting to hear anything about Him. Sometimes we "run" into a religion that appeases our corrupted consciences with a small obligation of duty, brief and limited church attendance, religious ritual, giving, being benevolent, or going to a confessional. We erroneously think that we will please God by performing these "religious works." We make a huge mistake when we assume that God thinks the same way we do because God does not think like us at all. This will be a very important lesson that will cause this book to make far more sense later on. God, through the prophet Isaiah, said,

For my thoughts are not your thoughts, nei-
ther are your ways my ways, saith the LORD.
For as the heavens are higher than the earth,
so are my ways higher than your ways, and
my thoughts than your thoughts. Isaiah 55:8-9

God's desire is to *renovate* our minds to think like Him. Paul wrote,

And be not conformed to this world: but be
ye transformed by the renewing of your mind,
that ye may prove what is that good, and
acceptable, and perfect, will of God. Romans 12:2

When we understand the underlying reason for divorce we can conclude that while God wants our marriages to remain unbroken, we do otherwise. And when we do otherwise, we demonstrate that we do not care what anyone else says or thinks, including God! However, that mind-set is not good, because it shows that our hearts are not malleable, even by God which is the main reason Jesus gave for divorce. After Jesus answered His disciples' first question about divorce by declaring that man should not separate those whom God has joined together in marriage, they asked a follow-up question.

"...Why did Moses then command to give
a writing of divorcement, and to put her
away?"

And that is when they received this lesson on hardheartedness from the Master Teacher:

He saith unto them, "Moses because of the hardness of your hearts <u>suffered</u> [permitted] you to put away your wives: but from the beginning it was not so." Matthew 19:7-8*

Divorce happens because at least the husband or the wife, or both have a hardened heart and refuses to change their position, no matter what. This hardness is what destroys the relationship. Unfortunately, God will hold each person accountable for his or her hard heart, unless of course he or she repents and allow God to soften him or her to the point of compassionate and loving reason when applicable. Only after God softens a heart can it be expected that after divorce, each person can freely acknowledge his or her individual fault where the marriage was concerned, demonstrating that a real change has taken place within. The mercy and grace of God certainly helps to bring that kind of change about. Later on we will discuss more about mercy and grace.

Biological Compatibility

No one can dispute that God's objective was not just companionship. He had another goal that He wanted achieved through the male/female marriage relationship which is evident in the following verse:

*And God blessed them, and God said unto
them, Be fruitful, and multiply, and replenish
the earth, and subdue it: and have dominion
over the fish of the sea, and over the fowl
of the air, and over every living thing that
moveth upon the earth*. Genesis 1:28

Notice the phrase, "God blessed them..." The
ability to procreate in the lifelong relationship is
a plus and is called "a blessing," that is, a special
grace and benefit which is the central purpose of the
will of God. The ability to procreate was no fluke or
coincidental happenstance. Procreation was the plan
– the objective – God's central idea when He created Adam's companion. He made her compatible in
every way for that purpose. He put something inside
of Eve that was complemented only by something
inside of Adam. He gave her ovaries that produce
eggs. Those ova would become active only when
they would come in direct contact with sperm cells
that were made inside of Adam's body. God also created an efficient means by which those cells and ova
would meet, without which the sperm cells and ova
all die within a few days. Many will argue against
this point, but God created the act of sexual intercourse mainly to promote procreation. Why? One
answer can be found here:

*Didn't the LORD make you one with your
wife? In body and spirit you are his. And
what does he want? Godly children from your
union*. Malachi 2:15 NLT

24

God's purpose is to fill the world with people who would live godly lives and worship Him. Gay relationships cannot produce children in any way at all, let alone make them Godly because such relationships are unholy and irreversibly sinful in the sight of God. A marriage ceremony cannot change the sinfulness of a gay relationship.

The sensation of intercourse is part of the procreation plan and an incentive to bring it about. God also created the desire to have companions, to reproduce, grow families, and enjoy life within the framework of those families. While there will be many who will disagree with this position also, this is about natural desires. Generally, with few exceptions, those desires are present within each of us. Will every couple who marry produce children? No. As a matter of fact, no one is obliged to marry or find a companion at all. And in procreation, the imperfections of our DNA due to Adam's sin causes flaws that result in birth problems, sometimes hindering or even preventing the reproductive processes altogether in some couples, because the existence of sin has rendered imperfect what was created as perfect. But despite all of that, the complementary biological compatibility of man and woman where procreation is concerned is indisputable. That physical complementary characteristic ideally makes lifelong companions of a man and a woman.

A Covenant Relationship

Finally, the marriage that takes place between a man and a woman takes place under a covenant. The covenant is a vow made before God by the man and the woman that commits them to lifelong faithfulness to each other. Adam said that a man must leave his parents and live with his wife in marital unity for the rest of their lives. Such an arrangement translates into protection, stability, and security for wives and the children who are born as a result the union.

Covenants are a serious matter with God. The relationship that we have with him as believers in Christ is a covenant relationship. In the covenant that God has made with us, He promises to keep His conditional promises of provision and salvation that He has made to us if we will simply obey Him. We learn how to obey Him through learning what He wants through His word and His will which we find explained in the bible. Since God will keep His covenant that he made with us, He wants us to be like Him and keep the covenants we make when we marry. When the promise to love, and cherish until death parts us is made, God expects those who make such a promise to keep it faithfully. How can we possibly hold God responsible to keep His conditional promises He made to us if we should sin against Him by breaking our covenant promise to remain with our spouse until death alone separates us?

The prophet Malachi confirmed that marriage is based in a covenant when God spoke through Him decrying the treacherous ways of the men of His people who trivially broke their covenants of marriage by saying:

> *"Yet you say, `For what reason?' Because the LORD has been a witness between you and the wife of your youth, against whom you have dealt treacherously, though she is your companion and your wife by covenant.* Malachi 2:14 NASU

Stability is important to a marriage in God's eyes because it is the foundation for Godly children, which is God's ultimate goal in marriage. God wants a man to be as faithful towards his wife and vice versa as He is towards us.

Chapter Two

A BRIEF OVERVIEW OF WHAT THE BIBLE TEACHES

*B*efore we can go on, it is necessary to understand a little of the purpose and intent of the bible itself. Generally, Americans are astute in almost every other subject, but a study of the bible escapes most Americans as a necessary discipline. This has been sometimes glaringly evident during game shows where biblical trivia is introduced. The contestants often are unaware of the answers to questions regarding even some of the most simple and common biblical subjects. Even some members of the clergy do not see the complete picture that the bible presents. Yet, the bible tells an important story – the story of sin and redemption – and the Old and New Testaments combine to tell that story. Failure to understand how the Old Testament figures in the entire scheme of the plan of God generally results in misinterpretation of scriptures and false doctrine.

The origin of sin will now be discussed to help establish the basis for the story of sin and redemption. In the previous chapter, we were made aware of how sin affects human life. Now we will discuss its origin, its inevitable consequences, and what God chose to do about it. Such understanding is necessary because we must deal with sex in two ways: sex as sin and sex as God intended it to be.

Temptation and Sin

When God created the world, He created Adam and gave him the responsibility of caring for the Garden of Eden. In the garden, He placed two trees from either of which the fruit was edible; the Tree of Life, and the Tree of the Knowledge of Good and Evil. There were a number of various other fruit trees available for food as well. God gave Adam permission to eat from any of the fruit trees except the one called the Tree of the Knowledge of Good and Evil. In that prohibition, it is evident that Adam had a free will and could choose whether to obey God, or to follow his own desires and decisions.

Initially, the Tree of the Knowledge of Good and Evil seemed to hold no special interest for Adam, and the commandment of God to leave it alone was sufficient for him. For a short while, he apparently managed not to be influenced by its existence at all. However, Adam needed a companion and God supplied her for him as stated in the previous chapter.

After she was created, Adam apparently passed along to her the commandment that God had given to him so that she too knew that God did not want them to eat from that particular tree. The Tree of the Knowledge of Good and Evil piqued Eve's curiosity more so than Adam's, drawing her to further ponder this tree and its forbidden fruit. As she did, another of God's creatures, the serpent, being aware of the meticulous attention that Eve paid to the tree, engaged her in conversation with devious intent.

He asked, "Did God *really* say that you must not eat from any tree of the garden?" She replied, "We may eat the fruit from any of the trees in the garden except from the one that is in the middle of the garden because God said that we must not eat from it or even touch it, or we will die." The serpent countered by saying, "You won't really die, because God knows that as soon as you eat from it your eyes will be opened, and you will be just like Him, knowing good and evil."[1]

But the serpent had lied and directly contradicted God's commandment about what the consequence would be for eating from the Tree of the Knowledge of Good and Evil. Suddenly, the idea about knowing good and evil was desirable to Eve, and now she wanted to know more about what that knowledge was and how it could enhance her being. The serpent made sure that Eve would follow through and eat from the tree by implying that God was purposely keeping back this wonderful secret of "good and evil" from both her and Adam because He was trying to prevent them from becoming like Him. The serpent also made it seem as if this knowledge would elevate their lowly status to a more lofty status like God's to the extent that they could become powerful like Him![2]

Now this is a perfect spot where we can learn more about Satan and his methods. One truth stands out here: God had given a very clear commandment, and then Satan came along and distorted the meaning of that clear commandment by introducing doubt as to what God actually meant by it. God had plainly commanded Adam not to eat from the tree of the Knowledge of Good and Evil, but after Adam had relayed the commandment to Eve, Satan came to her and stirred up doubt within her about the truthfulness of the commandment perhaps because she had not received it directly from God as did Adam. My paraphrase of the verse above is what I believe is the implication of the verse. Satan then went on to say *exactly the opposite* of what God had commanded them. He said, "You will not surely die, but instead you will become like God, knowing good and evil." God had said that they would die if they ate from The Tree of the Knowledge of Good and Evil, and Satan countered that they would not die, but rather that they would become more enlightened.

After Jesus came, He gave more light on Satan by teaching that Satan is a liar and the father of lies.[3] So what we learn of Satan is that He lies and distorts the truth of God in an attempt to contrarily influence men to believe the opposite of what God *plainly* commanded.

The erroneous information Eve received from the serpent gave her more impetus to sample this fruit that could give her knowledge and power and elevate her status. Overwhelmed by the temptation that was gnawing away at her internally, she picked the forbidden fruit and gobbled it down. Not feeling any physical effect as a result of eating, she located her husband Adam, and told him what she had done. Bringing him back to the tree, she picked a fruit for him and gave it to him, enticing him to do the same.[4] He ate the fruit and as soon as he had done so, both of them had a sudden surge of understanding of the magnitude of the error that they had just committed. They were so filled with shame until it had become very difficult for them to even face each other naked despite being husband and wife. But the dominant reason for their shame was their consciousness of the presence of God. They were aware of God's presence and they were attempting to hide the shame of their nudity from His sight. Therefore, in a futile attempt to deal with this newly discovered shame, they secured fig leaves and somehow lashed them together to put onto their bodies in a weak effort cover themselves.[5] They had discovered evil, and they now realized that what they had done was not good at all. In time, they would discover the severity of their actions.

God certainly knew what they had done. When He came near to them as the day cooled and drifted towards evening, they tried to hide from Him. God already knew where they were and why, but since He requires confession, He called for them.

"Adam, where are you?" called God.

"I'm hiding," answered Adam. "Hiding? Why?" queried God.

"Well, because I'm naked," replied Adam.

"Naked?" answered God with a question of His own. "How do you know that? Who told you that you were naked?" Silence. "Adam, did you eat from the tree that I told you not to eat from?" God also knew how they would react after eating from the tree.

"Well, the woman whom *you* gave to me brought the fruit to me, and I ate it," replied Adam. Adam blamed his sin on Eve *and* God.

"Oh? Eve! You did *what?*" demanded God.

"Well," replied Eve, "The serpent fooled me. That's why I ate it." Eve blamed her sin on the serpent. Then God turned and declared His judgment against the serpent – not because Eve sinned, but rather because he had lied to her. Now without going into any more detail, suffice it to say that the main consequence and punishment for man's disobedience to the command of God is death.[6] That is why the bible says:

> *For the wages of sin is death; but the gift of God is eternal life through Jesus Christ our Lord.* Romans 6:23

What Sin Really Is

Now here is where we can learn a not-so-well-known truth. Notice what brought the death penalty to Adam and Eve. The transgression that brought the sentence of death was not any of the traditional "biggies" that we all tend to categorize as "bad" and "evil" or the "worst of the worst," nor was it anything that is ordinarily considered harmful, destructive, abusive or violent. This truth helps to teach us what sin *really* is. Sin is disobedience to the command of God, regardless of how miniscule we think that the behavior, the offence, or the after-effects are. Any commission of it on our part makes us in God's eyes worthy and deserving of His judgment which is death. The bible further teaches that:

> *Whosoever committeth sin transgresseth also the law: for sin is the transgression of the law.* 1 John 3:4

When a person sins willfully as did Adam and Eve, he is showing no regard for the law of God as if the law of God never existed. The bible calls that a "transgression." When a person transgresses, that person is violating God's commandment. When people sin consistently every day, it is because their lifestyles disregard the law of God. According to the bible, to live that way is to live in unrighteousness.

When Adam and Eve sinned, they had disregarded the commandment that God had given them, showing complete contempt for it, and consequently introduced sin and death into the world. Herein is the reason Jesus died on the cross. He became our substitute and took the penalty of death for sin upon himself as though He were the one who violated all of God's commands. The bible confirms that truth by the following biblical passages:

> *But He was pierced through for our trans-gressions, He was crushed for our iniquities; the chastening for our well-being* (punishment that allows us to escape punishment) *fell upon Him, and by His scourging we are healed. All of us like sheep have gone astray, each of us has turned to his own way, but the LORD has caused the iniquity of us all to fall on Him.* Isaiah 53:5-6 NASU*

> *And according to the Law, one may almost say, all things are cleansed with blood, and without shedding of blood there is no forgive-ness.* Hebrews 9:22 NASU

Those passages are only two of numerous passages that confirm that Jesus died to take away our sins and thus negate the penalty that is otherwise due us so that we can receive eternal life. In order to prevent misconceptions that lead to dangerous false assumptions, one needs to do more personal prayerful and objective research. Such research sets the stage for the proper foundation for the understanding of the truth.

Although God's solution to the sin problem has been discussed, how does the bible go about identifying what acts are sin? The Torah (also called the Law of God) serves that purpose. The Torah can be found within the section of the bible which we call the Old Testament, which is probably the least understood section of the bible because we Gentiles are not immediately familiar with its subject matter, and it takes time and careful study and prayer to understand it. Now there has been much debate over whether or not the Old Testament is relevant to us today, and whether or not Christians are "under" the Old Testament or the New Testament only, and whether or not any discussion on the Old Testament is even necessary. The debate exists only because of the difficulty of understanding the message of the Old Testament, which again can be discovered by prayerful, objective study and a genuine desire for truth.

The Purpose of the Commandments

Many people mistakenly believe that keeping the Ten Commandments is the only responsibility of Christianity. While those ten are the first and the most basic of all the commandments, there were actually a total of 613 commandments presented by God to Israel. Jewish scholars further categorized them as 248 positive commandments, and 365 negative commandments. We call them "dos" and "don'ts." Now here is a question that has certainly brought on a storm of controversy: is it necessary for Christians today to follow the commandments, or were they given only to Jewish people? The bible does state that the Torah was written for all people, because it had a purpose. The Apostle Paul wrote,

Now we know that what things soever the law saith, it saith to them who are under the law: that every mouth may be stopped, and all the world may become guilty before God. Therefore by the deeds of the law there shall no flesh be justified in his sight: for by the law is the knowledge of sin. Romans 3:19-20

From those verses we discover that the Torah (the law) helps us to understand what sin is, and that even following and obeying all 613 commandments alone would still fail to bring justification (guiltlessness) before God, because attempting to follow those mandates alone is not good enough to secure forgiveness of sins, salvation, and eternal life because the Torah does not and cannot atone for, nor redeem anyone from sin, nor can it grant eternal life.[7] Now we can understand why it was necessary for Jesus to die for us. Remember: *"without the shedding of blood, there is no forgiveness for sin."*[8] So the Torah shows us what sin is, declares us all to be guilty sinners, and then teaches what will happen to us as a result of that guilt. Unfortunately, it cannot give eternal life to us. Notice also that the Torah has declared the entire world (that includes Gentiles) to be guilty before God. So the Torah leaves us with guilt without salvation.

A careful study of the Torah will reveal seven festivals that were celebrated in Israel each year. Each one of the festivals in some way depicts another step in God's total plan of salvation. The subject of the festivals is too complex to go into in detail here, but

I will briefly mention Yom Kippur, or the Day of Atonement.

The Mercy of God

Yom Kippur, or The Day of Atonement, literally means 'Day of Mercy.' On this day the High Priest would offer a bull and two goats—the bull for himself and one goat for the people's sins. The other goat was released and led into the wild.[9] The bull and the two goats were all symbolic of the work of Jesus Christ in the salvation process. One goat provided the symbol of mercy through atonement, and the other provided the symbol of the forgiveness of sins. While those two sacrifices teach several lessons about how God deals with our sins, we will only deal with one of them—the subject of mercy. Jesus' death not only provides forgiveness of sins, but His death also provides mercy for sinners. Mercy makes it possible to for all of us to continue to live despite our penchant to disregard God and ignore His righteous standards. Thus, people can commit some of the most heinous acts known to man because of the mercy that Jesus' death provides. Mercy allows us to continue to live, even as evil individuals, despite whatever acts we many have committed, although we may deserve to die instantly by God's standards and go directly into His judgment and eternal condemnation.Without the provision of mercy in atonement, absolutely no one could ever be saved at all. Because the blood of bulls and goats could not actually provide either mercy or forgiveness, this act of atonement had to be repeated in the Yom Kippur festival annually in order for God to continue to favor and bless Israel.[10] But the festival's real purpose was not to exalt itself, but to foretell about the atoning work of the Messiah Jesus, and about the merciful nature of God. So the bible really teaches us that regardless of how good we think we are to ourselves or to the rest of the world, our sins cannot be forgiven without the shed blood of the Lamb of God, Jesus Christ, and His blood cannot be applied without our intentionally exercising faith in Him to the point of purposefully making Him our supreme master (Lord) and teacher. One must become a lifelong disciple (pupil) of Jesus and live by His teachings each day.

Mercy in Eden

We learned earlier that Adam and Eve had been told that in the day that they would violate the command of God and eat from the Tree of the Knowledge of Good and Evil that they would die. After they violated God's command and had thus sinned, they sewed some fig leaves together and tried to cover themselves with them because they were ashamed to be naked in the presence of God, as well as in their own presence. Their feeble attempt to cover themselves was not sufficient. Instead, God slaughtered two animals, one for each of them and used the bloody animal skins to cover their bodies. Because the death of those two animals were of a substitutionary nature for Adam and Eve, God showed them mercy and allowed them to live on a while longer even though they deserved death.[11] They had received a tempo-rary covering for their sin, just as Israel had on the day of atonement.

Being "Good" Without Jesus is Evil

It is deceptive to think that living a "good life" (by man's concept of goodness) will earn for us sal-vation and eternal life which as explained previously are only acquired by forgiveness of sins through Jesus' blood. Even before receiving salvation, one must repent, which is an attitude of repulsion for having sinned against God, and then confess, which is agreeing with God that we have sinned against Him and that any judgment that He would bring upon us as a result of those sins is just and appropriate. It is by these means that one falls on the mercy of Jesus. After that, a person must make Jesus his master and faithfully follow His teachings. He said,

"It is the Spirit who gives life; the flesh profits nothing; the words that I have spoken to you are spirit and are life. John 6:63 NASU

Being "good" without repentance toward God and faith in Jesus Christ will not earn eternal life. God has already described to us through the prophet Isaiah what He thinks of our goodness outside of sal-vation in Christ. Isaiah said,

But we are all as an unclean thing, and all our righteousnesses are as filthy rags; and

we all do fade as a leaf; and our iniquities, like the wind, have taken us away. Isaiah 64:6

The Hebrew word for the phrase "filthy rags" is *idyim* and it refers to a soiled menstrual cloth which is not very flattering for anyone who thinks of himself as a good person before God. Yet, that is what God thinks of our goodness without Jesus. Anyone who is simply "good" but has not turned to Jesus for forgiveness of sins nor made Jesus his Master and teacher will not receive eternal life.

How the Torah Figures in All of This

So now, do we follow the Torah? Does Jesus' teachings supercede the Torah? Here is the answer: <u>all</u> of Jesus' teachings are all based on <u>all</u> of the Torah, because Jesus taught *righteousness*, which was the intent of the Torah. Righteousness is *right standing* with God.

For Christ is the end of the law for righteousness to every one that believeth. Romans 10:4

Let's restate that verse in a way that may be easier for us to comprehend:

The [revelation of] Messiah is the intent of the law, so that righteousness can be obtained by everyone who believes [in Him].

The ultimate goal of the law was and is to introduce sinful man to Jesus the Messiah so that he can acquire the righteousness of God which is unobtainable through the law alone. In order to accomplish its goal, the law had to identify sin. But what the Torah could not do as stated before is atone for sins committed. Thus, Christ died on the cross in order to remove the guilt of sins committed, and most importantly, to remove the penalty for sin—death—which is the consequence of Adam's sin that has come upon all of mankind.

> *Wherefore, as by one man sin entered into the world, and death by sin; and so death passed upon all men, for that all have sinned:* Romans 5:12

> *For if by one man's offence death reigned by one; much more they which receive abundance of grace and of the gift of righteousness shall reign in life by one, Jesus Christ. Therefore as by the offence of one judgment came upon all men to condemnation; even so by the righteousness of one the free gift came upon all men unto justification of life. For as by one man's disobedience many were made sinners, so by the obedience of one shall many be made righteous.* Romans 5:17-19

The answer to the question, "Do we follow the Torah?" is "Yes we do." How? We follow it by obeying Jesus. Here is why. In order for a person to be considered righteous by God, the Torah must be satisfied (fulfilled) by that person because the Torah is God's standard of righteousness. But it is extremely difficult for man to satisfy every single righteous demand of God's laws and even if he could, his efforts would not bring him everlasting life because the bible says,

> *[B]ecause by the works of the Law no flesh will be justified in His sight; for through the Law comes the knowledge of sin.* Rom 3:20 NASU*

When Jesus came to the earth, He did not change any of God's commandments of righteousness. Jesus himself said,

> *Think not that I am come to destroy the law, or the prophets: I am not come to destroy, but to fulfill.* Matthew 5:17

Jesus announced that He did not come to abolish the law, but to satisfy it. He accomplished that by satisfying the righteous requirements of the law which we are unable to satisfy.

The Torah can be divided into two parts: commandments we can satisfy, and commandments that we cannot satisfy. Now we can take the ones we can satisfy and also divide them into two parts: those that are practical, and those that are impractical. The ones that are practical are those that can be kept and practiced by us. Through those, we fulfill or satisfy some of the righteous demands of the law. But be warned that we must satisfy the entire law. The impractical are those precepts of the law which we cannot satisfy, because they have already been satisfied for us by the work of the Messiah, and any attempt of them would be unnecessarily redundant and not useful, such as slaughtering animals for sacrifices for sin, or bringing food sacrifices to an altar, or having incense burned on our behalf. Because Jesus sacrificed His life for us, those sacrifices are no longer necessary. The Torah's purpose with animal sacrifices was to teach us about the necessity of the blood sacrifice of Jesus for our sins. Thus Jesus satisfied the Torah there.

The law of week-long isolation of a female during menstruation is also impractical. In the Torah she was declared unclean during menses and had to purify herself while being separated from her family during that otherwise natural bodily process. Had she sat on a chair while menstruating, and then a family member later sat on the same chair, the chair and the other family member would also have been considered unclean at least until the evening. Even sexual intercourse with her husband during that time would render them both unclean for seven days.[12] Since she is now cleansed through Christ's blood, then a ritual ceremonial cleansing is unnecessary, for His blood cleanses her continually, menses or not, and she is no longer unclean during her period.

Other parts of the law that can be considered impractical are those which were designed to teach special lessons first to Israel, and afterwards to followers of Jesus. For example, Paul teaches from the law the following precept in Deuteronomy 25:4:

For it is written in the Law of Moses, "YOU SHALL NOT MUZZLE THE OX WHILE HE IS THRESHING." God is not concerned about oxen, is He? Or is He speaking altogether for our sake? Yes, for our sake it was written, because the plowman ought to plow in hope, and the thresher to thresh in hope of sharing the crops. If we sowed spiritual things in you, is it too much if we reap material things from you? 1 Corinthians 9:9-11 NASU

According to Paul, the precept is actually a commandment that has little bearing on oxen, but a greater purpose for ministers of the gospel. For the Jew under the old covenant, it was indeed a literal precept to keep. But its intent is much deeper because it is a lesson that teaches that no one, not even animals should work for nothing, how much more ministers of the Gospel who have a God-given responsibility of oversight for His people? Paul taught that from the beginning the precept was really aimed at apostles and ministers of the gospel of Jesus the Messiah who had a right to expect that the church would provide for their natural needs since they take the time and sacrifice their lives to provide for the church's spiritual needs.

Deuteronomy 22:9-12 is also a precept that has another intended meaning than that of its face value:

Thou shalt not sow thy vineyard with divers seeds: lest the fruit of thy seed which thou hast sown, and the fruit of thy vineyard, be defiled. Thou shalt not plow with an ox and an ass together. Thou shalt not wear a garment of divers sorts, as of woollen and linen together. Thou shalt make thee fringes upon the four quarters of thy vesture, wherewith thou coverest thyself.

God was not aiming only at trivial things such as planting different types of seeds together, or combining different types of fabrics together, or whether one plowed a field with an ox and a donkey as a team. God was using things that everyone at that time could understand to teach greater analogous truths to the Hebrew people about holiness and living separate from sin through the everyday acts of living. Those concepts were not only for them, but also for the followers of Jesus in our time—that righteous living cannot be mixed with sinful living and still be considered righteous. Our actions, lifestyles, and behavior must be pure before God by His standards.

The first message in the passage just quoted from Deutononomy 22:9-12 deal with planting grapes with other types of plants. Doing so would cause the flavor, nutrition, and possibly the healthiness of the grapes to be affected by the composition and characteristics of the other plant or plants with which the grapes were planted. Just as grapes can be affected by the intermingling of the roots of the other plants, the fruits of righteousness can be adversely affected if we mix our supposed righteous behaviors with unrighteous behaviors.

The second message deals not with combining different types of material into everyday clothing that we wear as some erroneously suppose, but with the tzit-tzit that Jewish men were commanded to wear. That God was talking about the tzit-tzit is clearly seen in the next verse (12) where God mentions the necessity of having fringes on the four corners of the garment. The tzit-tzit had to be made entirely of one type of material — either wool or linen (or even cotton). It was designed to remind them of the commandments of God and to not follow the ways and philosophies of the other nations (see also Numbers 15:38-41). Obeying the commandment symbolized that their obedience to the law of God was not to be mixed with the ungodly philosophies and practices of the world. In modern times, the talitt has replaced the tzit-tzit.

What About Food?

The food prohibitions are also impractical. Why? Because in the following passage, God showed the apostle Peter in a vision that He had cleansed all food that had previously been declared unclean:

On the morrow, as they went on their journey, and drew nigh unto the city, Peter went up upon the housetop to pray about the sixth hour: and he became very hungry, and would have eaten: but while they made ready, he fell into a trance, and saw heaven opened, and a certain vessel descending unto him, as it had been a great sheet knit at the four corners, and let down to the earth: wherein were all manner of fourfooted beasts of the earth, and wild beasts, and creeping things, and fowls of the air. And there came a voice to him, Rise, Peter; kill, and eat. But Peter said, Not so, Lord; for I have never eaten any thing that is common or unclean. And the voice spake unto him again the second time, What God hath cleansed, that call not thou common. Acts 10:9-15

Additionally, another passage states:

For every creature of God is good, and nothing to be refused, if it be received with thanksgiving: For it is sanctified by the word of God and prayer. I Timothy 4:4

God shows us in other biblical passages that He instituted the dietary laws as another way of teaching Israel and followers of Jesus about holy and pure living in a practical way using analogies which they understood. In doing so (through obedience) they would be holy to Him. Therefore He told them,

"Ye shall therefore put difference between clean beasts and unclean, and between unclean fowls and clean: and ye shall not make your souls abominable by beast, or by

fowl, or by any manner of living thing that creepeth on the ground, which I have separated from you as unclean. And ye shall be holy unto me: for I the LORD am holy, and have severed you from other people, that ye should be mine." Lev 20:25-26

Holiness is something that God wants from all of His people, and not just the Levitical priesthood as some erroneously believe. To the church, Peter wrote quoting from Leviticus 11:44:

As obedient children, do not be conformed to the former lusts which were yours in your ignorance, but like the Holy One who called you, be holy yourselves also in all your behavior; because it is written, "YOU SHALL BE HOLY, FOR I AM HOLY." 1 Peter 1:14-16 NASU

According to Peter, God wants us to live a lifestyle free from the mixture of lusts and evil desires that would otherwise control us, which is the intent of the analogous teaching on holiness in the dietary laws.

The well known practical commandments that we can satisfy are the ones that prohibit stealing, perjury, adultery, coveting, murder, idolatry, sexual sins, honoring God, respecting parents, along with a host of other concepts that deal with human relationships, behavior, interaction with others, and our relationship towards God.

The basis of the Torah is love. Paul wrote,

> *For this, Thou shalt not commit adultery,*
> *Thou shalt not kill, Thou shalt not steal, Thou*
> *shalt not bear false witness, Thou shalt not*
> *covet; and if there be any other command-*
> *ment, it is briefly comprehended in this*
> *saying, namely, Thou shalt love thy neigh-*
> *bour as thyself. Love worketh no ill to his*
> *neighbour: therefore love is the fulfilling of*
> *the law.* Romans 13:9-10

The most important commandment of love is the one that tells us to love God supremely. When Jesus taught this, He quoted Deuteronomy 6:5 saying,

> *And He said to him, " 'YOU SHALL LOVE*
> *THE LORD YOUR GOD WITH ALL YOUR*
> *HEART, AND WITH ALL YOUR SOUL,*
> *AND WITH ALL YOUR MIND.' 38 "This*
> *is the great and foremost commandment.*
> Matthew 22:37-38 NASU

Those who love God supremely will be willing to live by whatever commandment that He gives.

Traditions of External Purity

When the Pharisees wanted to accuse Jesus' disciples of wrongdoing for eating without first washing their hands according to the Talmudic tradition, Jesus showed them that they were misguided. They had asked, "Why do thy disciples transgress the tradition of the elders? For they wash not their hands when they eat bread."[13] Jesus then made a point that those teachings were the "tradition of the elders" but not the actual law of God. Those traditions were supposedly handed down as oral law by the elders of Moses' day, and then later written as the Talmud, which includes a multi-volume commentary on them that eventually resulted in things being taught alongside the Torah that God had actually never required, and that also tended to sometimes be contrary to commandments that God did require.[14] Because of that, Jesus countered their question with a question of His own: "Why do you yourselves transgress the commandment of God for the sake of your tradition?"[15]

Jesus had tried to convince them that the things that they considered important were not derived from the law of God, but rather from the traditions handed down and developed by men who were erroneously held in higher esteem than the law of God. He went on to show that failure to recognize those traditions would not defile anyone, by saying,

> . . .*Hear, and understand: Not that which goeth into the mouth defileth* (makes unclean) *a man; but that which cometh out of the mouth, this defileth a man. Matthew 15:10-11*

By that statement he taught that defilement is the result of evil behavior that originates from a defiled mind. He also tried to convince them that they were responsible to keep God's law rather than their Talmudic traditions because they had rejected the commandments of God which were important to spiritual well-being and righteousness in favor of their man-made traditions.

The book of Mark shows that Jesus' disciples also had trouble understanding what Jesus meant so they questioned Him again. Although He knew that He had made His teaching clear to them the first time, they did not understand and His reply seemed to show some agitation because he said:

And he saith unto them, Are ye so without understanding also? Do ye not perceive, that whatsoever thing from without entereth into the man, it cannot defile him; Because it entereth not into his heart, but into the belly, and goeth out into the draught (pronounced "draft"), *purging all meats?* Mark 7:18-19*

The phrase "purging all meats" means that regarding unclean animals, Jesus' statement declared that they were now clean and free from ritual impurity. The New American Standard Updated Bible says it like this:

And He said to them, 'Are you so lacking in understanding also? Do you not understand that whatever goes into the man from outside cannot defile him, because it does not go into his heart, but into his stomach, and is eliminated?" (Thus He declared all foods clean) Mark 7:18-19

Jesus' declaration meant that eating foods once declared unclean cannot defile a person spiritually, but rather the evil practices such as any ungodly behavior, sinful actions, evil thoughts, pride, slander, adultery, and sexual sins, spiritually defiles a person before God. Jesus' death would seal the declaration that foods once called unclean would become acceptable for consumption without defilement.

One more example of another impractical law is the one where God commanded all males to appear before Him three times a year in Jerusalem during the feasts.[16] For many men in other parts of the world today, that would be an expensive and time consuming proposition. For others, it is impossible. Yet, the Torah requires those convocations. But Jesus vicariously appeared in Jerusalem before God for all men.[17] So in short, the difficult demands of the Torah are satisfied in Jesus. The other practical laws such as the ones mentioned above are still required by us to be obeyed. So as a result, we keep the righteousness of the entire law of God through faith in Jesus Christ.[18]

The Blessings of Obedience to God

Believers in Christ do not obey God's commandments in order to earn eternal life, because grace has already provided that for us as a gift. We obey them because we have already received salvation and eternal life as a gift from God through Jesus Christ, and because we are new creations in Christ through the new birth, and also because we love Him with all our hearts and desire to please Him. Furthermore, we obey the commandments by obeying the principles that Jesus and his apostles taught, because they are all based on the Torah. Since believers are saved by grace, we do not have to try to earn eternal life by our behavior because eternal life cannot be earned or purchased. Instead, it has been signed, sealed, and delivered to us by our gracious heavenly Father through Jesus Christ because of the Father who loves us and wants us to be saved. But that grace does not preclude obedience to the laws of behavior and morality that He wants us to live by. Grace only works in righteousness!

> *. . . so that, as sin reigned in death, even so grace would reign through righteousness to eternal life through Jesus Christ our Lord.* Romans 5:21 NASU

The Torah: The Standard of Judgment

Since the Torah requires those things of everyone, then all people are responsible for those things and must answer to God as to why they have not done them or why they chose to live contrary to them. Outside of the blood of Jesus, no one stands a chance for salvation. When God judges the world, he will judge it on the basis of the Torah. Revelation 20:12 says,

> *And I saw the dead, small and great, stand before God; and the books were opened:*

and another book was opened, which is the book of life: and the dead were judged out of those things which were written in the books, according to their works.

If God is going to judge men for the sins they have committed, what would be His basis? It would have to be his Torah. Romans 3:19 which was quoted earlier says that the Torah has declared everyone to be sinners and accountable to it before God, and verse 20 says that the Torah shows us what sin is. So it appears that all people who come before God without Christ will be judged by the Torah. But for those who have repented of their sins and have been born again, the righteous demands of the Torah will have been fulfilled on their behalf because they come before God redeemed (purchased) from sin by the blood of Jesus who is the Messiah and Lamb of God who has satisfied the law for us.

Understanding the Bible

The bible is an awesome and unique book. The answers to many interpretation difficulties can be found within its pages and if one seeks and trust God, He will provide the answers. Just as the disciples sometimes asked questions of Jesus about the meaning of what he taught,[19] we can do the same thing. God will certainly show us anything we want to know where truth is concerned. If He would not do that, he would not be reliable. It's rather silly to believe that God, an all-wise creator, wants us to know truth but is unable or unwilling to show it to us when we are asking for it. At the same time we must be teachable and ready to accept the truth that He shows us which is a very difficult proposition for human nature.

The best way to understand biblical truth is to listen to teachers whose lifestyles exemplify a genuine Godly standard, and then develop disciplines of personal study and prayer. A good example of that is presented by the Bereans who, after listening to the apostle Paul's teachings, engaged themselves in personal study and prayer to determine the truthfulness of the teachings that he had presented. They were considered "noble" for doing so.[20]

A good rule to follow where personal study is concerned is that if the bible contradicts your perceptions, then give the greater weight to the bible. During those times when we do not understand the whys of a particular biblical teaching, we must ask God to clarify for us the reasons for those concepts just as the disciples sometimes asked Jesus for clarification. Without the potential to receive truth, it would be impossible for us to receive eternal life for we would end up being lost in Satan's lies.

When we understand what sin is, then we can understand why and how the bible identifies certain sexual relationships as sinful.

Chapter Three

WHAT THE BIBLE REVEALS ABOUT MARRIAGE

It is impossible to speak of sex from a biblical point of view and not include marriage in the discussion because where God is concerned, the two are inseparable. When God gave the Israelites his ordinances for living, he mandated some guidelines for marriage that may be surprising and even a little foreign to most of us here in the 21st century. We will honestly deal with them at this time.

Now when we study scripture, that study will eventually reveal two conflicting perspectives—what God wants vs. what people want. The controversy exists because there are those who do not believe in God at all, those who have their own opinions about God, those who are not concerned about God's perspective, and finally, those who will not believe what anyone will say about what God wants, even if it can be biblically substantiated, because they are not interested in what God wants. Then there are those who think they know what God wants but are mistaken. Adding to that confusion, since there are various religious persuasions and beliefs and numerous opinions about the bible, it becomes increasingly difficult for everyone to come to a consensus about what the bible actually teaches. There are those who approach the bible literally, and then there are those who approach the bible symbolically. Then there are people who take a strict historical-critical approach, in which they attempt to clarify the difficulty of biblical understanding by looking at the historical periphery of the scripture in question. A correct approach will include a balance of all three so that the genuinely symbolic is not taken literally, and the historic concepts are not taken out of context and misapplied, while the literal is not ignored and neglected.

Even when the truths of the bible are correctly taught in churches, many people who need to hear those truths may not be present. They may also fail to do the kind of personal bible study that could lead them to truthful conclusions. The purpose of this book is to guide people to the truth of marriage and sexuality as presented by the bible, or at least to impart information that may pique their interest and ultimately cause them to ponder and objectively research the bible for better understanding on those subjects.

Incestuous Marriages

Biblical information on marriage is first introduced in the book of Genesis. Man began to make decisions on marriage long before God had given all of His righteous guidelines about it. Initially, the only information on marriage that existed was the precedent that God had set in creating a woman to become Adam's lifelong companion. Immediately after that, speaking with the mind of God, Adam, the human father of all of us, gave the law that stated that a man must leave his parents, join with his wife, and then remain with her in a lifelong relationship of oneness.[21] A couple of chapters later, Genesis 4:17 indicates that Cain had married a wife. For many in modern times, this was a perplexing problem because it was not immediately apparent to them where Cain's wife had come from. The question was raised in the famous Scope's trial that pit the theory of evolution against creationism in the legal arena.[22] The trial opened the door for secular liberalism by giving Christianity a very serious legal challenge which was a harbinger of things to come. The problem of where Cain's wife came from is not that difficult at all. While some may not agree, the most reasonable and sensible answer to where Cain's wife came from is found in verse 4 of Chapter 5 in the book of Genesis:

And the days of Adam after he had begotten Seth were eight hundred years: and he begat sons and daughters. . .

Adam had other sons and *daughters*. While the idea of incest is to us unthinkable, it is the only logical and reasonable conclusion that can be reached as to the origin of Cain's wife. Besides that, other than the precedent of man and woman, God had not given any other laws regarding incest as He had done in later times. Besides, how else could man have procreated on the planet in those early post-creation years except by brothers marrying sisters or other close relatives such as cousins and nieces? This is further evidenced when Abraham had settled in a place called Gerar with his wife Sarah. Abimelech the ruler saw her and wanted to take her to become his wife. Abraham, fearing that he would be killed if he revealed that Sarah was his wife, chose to protect himself and say that she was his sister.[23] But she in fact was his sister because she and Abraham had the same biological father, but different mothers.[24]

Another fact revealed here now that is foreign and perhaps difficult for today's Christians to accept or understand is that their father, Terah, also had another wife. The subject of polygamy will be discussed a little more in the next six sections. So it is reasonable then to conclude that Cain had married one of his sisters and then migrated to the land of Nod with her.

Here is an interesting scientific fact that can be applied to these early intra-familial relationships. I am no expert on this subject, but based on what is told to us today from those who study DNA, if siblings produce offspring, the health or physical well-being of the offspring is at risk due to certain weaknesses of the related parents' genes that are passed along to their offspring. Evidently, human DNA at creation was at its peak, perhaps accounting for the fact that people could live for several hundred years. But as mating between siblings and close family members continued, the genetic material deteriorated to the point where men could only consistently live to nearly 100 years or just over that before expiring. People had also spread out geographically so that the closeness in relations widened over a greater area and genetic weaknesses shifted to different areas in the human genome in different population and family groups. Over time, the number of females proliferated on the earth to the extent that men did not have to opt only for those with whom they were closely related. Had human DNA began like it is now, mankind probably would never have survived to the extent we do today. God allowed incestuous marriages at least until He gave the Torah on Mount Sinai.

Polygamous Marriages

Earlier, we learned that it is a possiblilty that Abraham's father, Terah, had more than one wife at one time. Two of his children, Abram and Sarai, eventually married. But in Genesis 4:19, we learn that Lamech also had two wives, thus revealing the first biblical account of polygamy.

And Lamech took unto him two wives: the name of the one was Adah, and the name of the other Zillah.

While we in modem times have decried polygamy, God apparently allowed it to happen without retribution. As a matter of fact, the Torah later accounted for it. Here is an example:

> *If a man have two wives, one beloved, and another hated, and they have born him children, both the beloved and the hated; and if the firstborn son be hers that was hated: Then it shall be, when he maketh his sons to inherit that which he hath, that he may not make the son of the beloved firstborn before the son of the hated, which is indeed the firstborn:* Deuteronomy 21:15-16

Polygamy may not be the ideal marital relationship, but God certainly allowed, validated and even legislated it in those days, and it is possible that He may even tolerate it to a limited extent today. But before we explore that possibility, let's look at some additional biblical accounts of polygamy.

Abram's wife Sarai, gave her handmaid Hagar, to be a concubine—a servant-wife—to Abraham so that Hagar would bear a child that she, Sarai, could mother since she could not become pregnant.[25] So the purpose of that arrangement was for Hagar to be a surrogate mother for a Sarai's child, and there was neither condemnation nor judgment from God on the matter. As a matter of fact, God eventually blessed Hagar and Abraham's son Ismael with a special blessing.[26]

Long before Abram (he was named Abram before God changed his name to Abraham[27]) was born, the bible in Genesis gives an account on polygamy and violence that provoked God to send a flood to destroy all living beings and creatures except Noah, his family, and the animals and other creatures that were taken onto the ark by the commandment of God. The circumstances around the activities that initiated the judgment are found in the following passages:

Genesis 6:1-3 Now it came about, when men began to multiply on the face of the land, and daughters were born to them, that the sons of God saw that the daughters of men were beautiful; and they took wives for themselves, whomever they chose. Then the LORD said, "My Spirit shall not strive with man forever, because he also is flesh; nevertheless his days shall be one hundred and twenty years."

Genesis 6:12-13 God looked on the earth, and behold, it was corrupt; for all flesh had corrupted their way upon the earth. 'Then God said to Noah, "The end of all flesh has come before Me; for the earth is filled with violence because of them; and behold, I am about to destroy them with the earth." NASU

There is a lot of speculation as to who the sons of God were. Some think that they were fallen angels. Additionally, it is believed that those larger human beings (the Nephilim) were the offspring of marital unions between those angelic beings, and mortal human beings.[28] Another theory held by many Jewish interpreters says that the sons of God were quality human beings who married lower quality human beings, thus accounting for the rise in corruption.[29] Without going into too much detail, I for one, believe that they are simply what we have called angels, who were created to serve man for God's purposes,[30] who in this case overstepped their boundaries and involved themselves in activities that God had forbidden them to involve themselves in, thus sinning against God in the process. They were sons of God because like Adam, their creation was direct and individual and not by procreation like Adam's offspring. Thus, they were physically made like us in every way, yet they were also endowed with supernatural abilities unlike us. When they appeared to men, they appeared to look like men which is why when they appeared they were called "men," but at the same time there was probably some kind of defining quality about them that stood out unlike men. I also believe that the Nephilim were their offspring that was the result of their marital unions with the women of earth.

Other biblical passages that refer to "sons of God" are:

Now there was a day when the sons of God came to present themselves before the LORD, and Satan came also among them. Job 1:6

Again there was a day when the sons of God came to present themselves before the LORD,

*and Satan came also among them to present
himself before the LORD.* Job 2:1

*When the morning stars sang together, and
all the sons of God shouted for joy?* Job 38:7

*...for they cannot even die anymore, because
they are like angels, and are sons of God,
being sons of the resurrection.* Luke 20:36
NASU

The sons of God seemed to be angels who abandoned their original mode of existence and behaved
violently like earthly men in the wanton desire and
craving for wives and sex and participated in or initiated the violence that accompanied that lust. Why is
that, you ask? The only way we can truly love and
serve God is if we have a choice not to. The same
would be true of the angels. They were all given the
choice not to serve God and many of them took that
choice. That choice is an indication of the existence
of free will.

Based on the passage it seems that the rise in
corruption centered around all the polygamous marriages and the violence. One reason for that violence
could very well have been the quest of men to marry
as many females as they desired. Perhaps that insa-
tiable desire led to those angels who were called 'the
sons of God' getting involved to the extent that they
also perpetrated violence. Suppose a female was
already married; if another wanted her badly enough
he might conspire to seize her using his power for

violence, force, or perhaps murder. Going forward, Abraham feared exactly that—being killed for his wife Sarai. Perhaps the quest for the most appealing females available, whether they were already married or not, resulted in the most severe violence, certainly a plausible reason that God would have become completely frustrated with His creation and move to cleanse it from those influences, and especially from the hybrid mixture of the offspring of the angels and the women. The angels being more powerful than the men would have left the men at a severe disavantage as well. Since the angels' involvement would have been severely damaging to God's creation, He was left with no choice but to cleanse it and start over and imprison the angels to keep them from doing it again.[31]

Levirate Marriage

As stated previously, after the Torah was given, some allowances were made within it for a man to have more than one wife which is evidenced by the guidelines that were given. For example, in the Law of the Levirate Marriage, it was required of a man to become a surrogate father for a brother who died if that brother died before his wife could conceive his child. The word Levirate comes from the Latin *levir* meaning "the husband's brother."[32] The first instance of this was seen long before the giving of the Torah in Genesis chapter 38. Somehow it had already become a part of the Hebrew culture that a man had the responsibility of making sure that his brother's name was carried on, despite his untimely demise. In that instance, Judah had found a wife named Tamar for his firstborn son Er, who had suddenly died in retribution from God as a result of his wicked lifestyle, whatever that may have been. Judah then went to his next son Onan, and asked him to take Tamar as a wife and conceive a child with her for his dead brother. Although Onan took her as a wife, he angrily withdrew himself during intercourse with her and discarded his ejaculate on the ground knowing that the first child would not officially be his. God, displeased with Onan's action, caused him also to die prematurely. Judah then told Tamar to go back home and live with her father until Shelah, his next son in line, was old enough for her to be given to him as a wife. In that account we can see the concept of the Levirate Law working long before God actually gave it as a commandment to Israel. The Levirate law was good for a widow. Because of the culture, her being a widow could easily cause her to end up very alone, poor, and even homeless in old age. Not many would want to marry her, and being childless, she would be completely helpless in old age if she had little or no family.

After a considerable period of time, Judah had forgotten his promise to Tamar. Shelah had grown up, but Tamar had not been given to him as a wife. Then Judah's wife died. Shrewdly, Tamar made herself unrecognizable and appeared as a prostitute by the side of the road so Judah could see her, probably figuring that she could probably get his attention because of his sexual need due to the death of his wife. Her plot worked. Not recognizing her because of her disguise, he had hired her for intercourse and promised her a goat for payment. As a good faith pledge until he had paid off his goat debt, he gave her his staff, and his cord that was around his neck that had a signet ring on it which was used to validate his legal affairs.[33]

A short time later, Judah sent his servant back with a goat to the spot where he had encountered her in order to pay her so that he could get back his staff and his signet cord. But when the servant got to the place, she was gone. The servant searched for her and inquired of different people who were in the area, but no one had recalled ever seeing a prostitute there at all. The servant returned with the goat and reported to Judah that there was no such woman there bearing the description that he had given.

The sexual encounter had caused Tamar to become pregnant, and because she was unmarried, the town gossip about her was that she had "played the harlot." Judah, angered by the things he had heard about her, and considering her to be reserved for his son Shelah, commanded her to be burned. She however, produced the evidence that she had actually conceived his child by demonstrating that she was impregnated by the owner of the staff and signet ring. Embarrassed, he correctly concluded that he was more at fault than she was because he had failed to carry out the promise that he had made to her concerning his son Shelah, and she had actually looked forward to the fulfillment of that promise. In addition to that failure, he was considering executing her for the same act that he had committed. Although God did not intervene at the time, we know that God has never justified prostitution. The twin children born to Tamar were credited to Judah.[34]

Levirate Law

After the giving of the Torah, an explicit command was given by God with respect to Levirate Marriage. It said:

If brethren dwell together, and one of them die, and have no child, the wife of the dead shall not marry without unto a stranger: her husband's brother shall go in unto her, and take her to him to wife, and perform the duty of an husband's brother unto her. And it shall be, that the firstborn which she beareth shall succeed in the name of his brother which is dead, that his name be not put out of Israel. And if the man like not to take his brother's wife, then let his brother's wife go up to the gate unto the elders, and say, My husband's brother refuseth to raise up unto his brother a name in Israel, he will not perform the duty of my husband's brother. Then the elders of his city shall call him, and speak unto him: and if he stand to it, and say, I like not to take her; Then shall his brother's wife come unto him in the presence of the elders, and loose his shoe from off his foot, and spit in his face, and shall answer and say, So shall it be done

> *unto that man that will not build up his brother's house. And his name shall be called in Israel, The house of him that hath his shoe loosed.* Deuteronomy 25:5-10

It is indeed possible that the brother (or nearest of kin) could have been already married, and unwilling to share his current inheritance to his children with any more children, so he could refuse—but not without the stigma that the refusal seemed to carry. On the other hand, he could simply marry the woman and end up with another wife. The levirate law of God made such a provision.

In chapters 3 and 4 of the book of Ruth, we see an instance of the Levirate Marriage law at work. Naomi, a Jewish widow had two sons, Mahlon and Chilion, the offspring of her late husband Elimelech, who had both interracially married with a Moabite woman. Both men died and the women were widowed and left childless. Naomi compelled them both to go back to their own people. She made an interesting comment that she had no more sons to give to them, an obvious reference to the Levirate Law. She further alluded to the law when she queried that even if she got married and immediately conceived, would these two young women be willing to wait until her sons were grown, provided that she even had sons? One of them, Orpah, reluctantly agreed with Naomi and returned to Moab. But the other one, Ruth, refused to leave declaring that Naomi's people (the Jews) would be her people, Naomi's God would be her God, and where Naomi died, she would die there too, and be buried there. Ruth's loyalty was not missed by a wealthy relative, Boaz, in whose field she went to glean the "corners of the harvest."[35] After meeting Ruth, he treated her with extreme kindness because of her loyalty towards Naomi. Naomi identified Boaz as a nearest of kin who could possibly be a kinsman redeemer under Levirate Law towards Ruth and take her as a wife. Now there was a closer relative than Boaz who had the first right to take Ruth as a wife.[36] When he learned that in addition to inheriting Elimelech's field he also had to marry Ruth as a kinsman redeemer, he refused saying:

> . . . *I cannot redeem it for myself, lest I mar mine own inheritance: redeem thou my right to thyself; for I cannot redeem it.* Ruth 4:6

This unnamed relative already had a wife and children and did not want to complicate their inheritance by taking in another wife. Thus, the Levirate Law allowed for a man to marry his dead relative's widow even if he was already married. The Torah allowed for polygamous marriages and women went along with it and did not contend against it.

King David and King Solomon

King David, a man after God's own heart by His estimation,[37] had more than one wife. His first wife was Michal, the daughter of King Saul. She became his wife after King Saul reneged on his first promise to reward David with his oldest daughter Merab for

killing the giant Goliath.[38] Because he was jealous
of the accolades being given to David by the people,
Saul decided to require a difficult dowry of David,
hoping that he would be killed trying to obtain it.
Saul proposed to give his younger daughter Michal
to David if he could kill 100 enemy Philistines and
as proof deliver their penises as a dowry to him. God
was with David however, and he subsequently turned
in 200 instead![39] King Saul reluctantly kept his end
of the bargain and allowed David to marry Michal.

2 Samuel 3:2-3, shows us that King David had
eventually acquired at least six more wives. They
are named in those two verses along with the children they bore for him while Michal is not named
there because she had no children.[40] Thus David had
already married seven wives when he encountered
Bathsheba, the wife of Uriah the Hittite who was a
very loyal soldier in the army of Israel. David's lust
for Bathsheba caused her to become impregnated by
him while her husband was away at war and eventually led the king to misuse his authority by having
Uriah strategically misplaced in an area of battle in
which he was unqualified so that he could be killed.[41]
After Uriah's death, King David married Bathsheba
in an effort to cover up their adulterous one night
stand. But God was not happy with what David had
done, although He later gave David mercy for the
sins he committed.[42] But as God scolded David, He
made the following comment:

> . . . *I anointed thee king over Israel, and*
> *I delivered thee out of the hand of Saul;*

And I gave thee thy master's house, and thy master's wives into thy bosom, and gave thee the house of Israel and of Judah; and if that had been too little, I would moreover have given unto thee such and such things. 2 Samuel 12:7-8

God said to David that He would have given him more of "these" if it was thought that what he had was not enough. God had given David Saul's wives, although David did not want them, and it appears that He would have also given David more wives if he had wanted them. There was no need for him to take another man's wife as he had done. King David's behavior sounds similar to what the sons of God may have done when violence accompanied their acquisition of wives.

King Solomon, David's son, was certainly not a little sheepish when it came to acquiring wives. He had 700 wives and princesses, and 300 concubines.[43] Solomon had sinned because God had already commanded that an Israelite king must never use his power to over-accumulate wives to himself because of the potential to be turned away from worshipping Him which is exactly what happened to Solomon.[44] God had directly warned Solomon to leave the foreign women alone because of the potential for idolatrous influence.[45] But Solomon was engaged in a personal quest to discover, using his wisdom, what could give a man maximum pleasure in return for his labor on earth. So in the process, he fulfilled all of his desires and held nothing back in his quest including bringing every woman he desired into his harem.[46]

Unfortunately, his quest caused him to actually abandon wisdom and sin against God because just as God had forewarned, King Solomon, in order to please his non-Jewish wives, began to build shrines for their idols.[47]

Thus the law of God allowed a man to have more than one wife without condemnation and polygamy did exist with God's blessing, in spite of our present position that the ideal marriage is one man married to one woman.

The New Testament and Polygamy

Apparently, there has been no time in history where there were not men who had more than one wife. The New Testament does not specifically say anywhere that a man should not have more than one wife at all. It does seem to imply the ideal of a man having only one wife, while perhaps indirectly acknowledging that polygamous marriages existed. In the previous chapter, we saw where Jesus gave his teaching on divorce and made it clear that divorce was never an option considered by God, but that it prevailed because of hard-heartedness. It can also be presumed true from New Testament teaching that the ideal relationship is one man/one woman. Yet, polygamous marriages did exist in New Testament times although monogamous marriages seemed to be prevalent.

The Apostle Paul, writing by the inspiration of the Holy Spirit, wrote in the monogamous sense when teaching marriage. He wrote:

> *Nevertheless, to avoid fornication, let every man have his own wife, and let every woman have her own husband.* 1 Corinthians 7:2

But here is where I believe that the Apostle Paul and the Holy Spirit acknowledges the existence of polygamy. Although there are different schools of thought on this passage, I believe it is a clear reference to the existence of polygamy where it says:

> *A bishop then must be blameless, the husband of one wife* . . . 1 Timothy 3:2

And there is another passage regarding deacons:

> *Let the deacons be the husbands of one wife, ruling their children and their own houses well.* 1 Timothy 3:12

No doubt God wants church leaders to be a prime example of the ideal God inspired marriage relationship which makes perfect sense. It makes more sense because a person in leadership by his position and influence could manipulate a lot of females. This prohibition certainly keeps this area under control and is protection for vulnerable females who are in need of love, proper guidance, and companionship while looking for genuine spiritual leadership. It prevents them from being put in a position where they could be selfishly used, and it also protects a leader from himself where he could easily lose the central focus of his mission due to the continued distraction of available females which is the mistake made by both kings David and Solomon. It is quite possible that a man of spiritual influence and leadership could be diverted from his true calling and multiply wives to himself even to the extent that King Solomon did. The prohibition against church leaders engaging in polygamy also influences all men to be monogamous who may aspire to church leadership so that they can be available for God's service without distraction.

I firmly believe that the bible demonstrates that the ideal marital relationship is that of one man/one woman, and besides, it is illegal in the United States to have more than one wife, which is a product of Christian influence. Hence, the legal system in our country enforces the Godly ideal of monogamous marriage. But at the same time, I do not believe that in countries where polygamy is allowed that a man needs to dump all but one of his legal wives if he came to know Christ Jesus as his Savior. I am sure that God would accept that man and all of his wives by grace just as He accepted David and all of his wives. God had even mercifully accepted the marriage of David and Bathsheba despite the way that their relationship transpired. Thus David said,

Blessed is he whose transgression is forgiven, whose sin is covered. Blessed is the man unto whom the LORD imputeth not iniquity, and in whose spirit there is no guile. Psalms 32:1-2

Precedents Never Set

One other precedent that was never biblically established is that of a woman and several husbands. This goes back to the fact that the woman was made for the man, and not vice-versa. It was also a concept that was strictly forbidden by the Torah. On that subject, Paul wrote:

Know ye not, brethren, (for I speak to them that know the law,) how that the law hath dominion over a man as long as he liveth? For the woman which hath an husband is bound by the law to her husband so long as he liveth; but if the husband be dead, she is loosed from the law of her husband. So then if, while her husband liveth, she be married to another man, she shall be called an adulteress: but if her husband be dead, she is free from that law; so that she is no adulteress, though she be married to another man. Romans 7:1-3

Paul taught that the Torah did not allow a woman to have more than one husband. If a married woman was also married to another man, she was called an adulteress by the law of God. But that was not true for the man. He could be married to another woman *without* being called an adulterer.

In addition, the man had always been considered the head of the marriage relationship, and the will of God is that his wife be submissive to him. Submissive does not mean subservient, and neither is submission a bad thing. Submissiveness is a quality of humility that allows for continuity in any relationship, whether family or business. It is a quality that exalts a wife and mother greatly, and secures the blessing of God upon her and her family. Jesus taught that submission is a place of power and not weakness. God considers the greatest person to be the one who voluntarily serves,[48] and He also promises to highly exalt any person who is submissive and humble.[49]

As far as the headship of the family is concerned, it was God who set that standard that the husband would be head of the marriage after Adam and Eve had sinned by saying:

> . . . *I will greatly multiply thy sorrow and thy conception; in sorrow thou shalt bring forth children; and thy desire shall be to thy husband, and he shall rule over thee.* Genesis 3:16

So we can conclude that it is God who set the hierarchy of the family relationship. We can also conclude then that even though God created one woman for Adam, the Torah had no objection for men who married more than one wife. But we can presume from Paul and Genesis 3:16 that the Torah did object to a woman having more than one husband.

When Jesus taught on marriage, He spoke of a man/woman relationship, which without doubt agrees with the precedent that God had established in the garden of Eden. Additionally, polygamy seems to be a part of the burden of the curse that women had to bear thanks to Eve's sin. Apparently, since Eve's sin was lack of obedience to God through the lack of submission to the simple instruction of her husband, her lot was to atone for that by total obedience and submission to her husband. The Torah added to that by allowing women to be put into some very humiliating circumstances with almost no legal recourse at all. The ordinances of Levirate Law and polygamy are two examples of ordinances that in modern opinion, seemed to work disproportionately against women but were nevertheless required to be obeyed. When Jesus died, he canceled out those kinds of ordinances and brought a new covenant of equity to the woman through His atonement. Paul said:

And you, being dead in your sins and the uncircumcision of your flesh, hath he quickened together with him, having forgiven you all trespasses;
Blotting out the handwriting of ordinances that was against us, which was contrary to us, and took it out of the way, nailing it to his cross; Colossians 2:13-14

Not every ordinance of the Law worked against man because the main purpose of the Law was to teach the righteousness of God. But those that did (those of menstruation, oozing skin sores, uncleanness due to childbirth, or the woman who was overpowered sexually being married to her attacker, etc.) were canceled out by Jesus' death on the cross so that we could receive salvation through His grace, rather than works.

Same Sex Relationships

No precedent was *ever* set by God in scripture regarding same-sex marriage. No scripture anywhere supports, implies, or validates same sex relationships or marriages. No biblical example is given anywhere of two men being wed together, or of two women being wed together, or of same-sex engagements, or of a man being given to another man in marriage, or of a woman being given to another woman in marriage, or of any romantic interests between same sex individuals whose relationship were approved by God or validated. There is no instruction anywhere in the bible that teaches a same-sex couple on how to live in or maintain such a relationship. Instead, whenever and whereever same-sex sex is mention in scripture, it is repudiated and condemned. That fact is irrefutable.

Chapter Four

THE OLD TESTAMENT AND SEX

*W*e cannot discuss sex from a biblical perspective without discussing marriage, and likewise we cannot discuss marriage without discussing sex. So to begin this chapter, we will explore the Hebrew root word *zanah* that is sometimes translated in various places in Old Testament scripture as *fornication, whoring,* or *harlot.*

Vine's Expository Dictionary of Old Testament Words, gives us a four-part definition of that root as:

"To go a whoring, commit fornication, be a harlot, serve other gods."

Vine's goes on to explain that *zanah* is the term that has indicated prostitution all through Israel's history and that while it translates as fornication committed either by a male or a female, it rarely referred to sexual impropriety by a male. Vine's further states that the main reason for that disparity is that the word was analogous to the spiritual prostitution of idolatry in forsaking God, which can be more easily symbolized by a woman forsaking her husband.[50] As a result, numerous analogies have been derived from that usage as it relates to Israel's relationship with God.

As we look at the definition and biblical usage of the word *zanah*, we see that it can refer to any of two things: illicit sexual activity (whether for pay or for free), or idolatry which is always considered spiritual prostitution against God. Thus, the word is always a sexual term regardless of whether it is used in the figurative or the literal application.

Various Laws of Sexual Conduct
Fornication

Now when the Torah was given, God gave specific laws of sexual conduct to Israel. Some of those laws are found beginning at Deuteronomy chapter 22:13, giving us the first lessons in a series of the Torah's teaching on human sexuality.

If any man take a wife, and go in unto her, and hate her, And give occasions of speech against her, and bring up an evil name upon her, and say, I took this woman, and when I came to her, I found her not a maid (virgin). Then shall the father of the damsel, and her mother, take and bring forth the tokens of the damsel's virginity unto the elders of the city in the gate: And the damsel's father shall say *unto the elders, I gave my daughter unto this man to wife, and he hateth her, And, lo, he hath given occasions of speech against her, saying, I found not thy daughter a <u>maid</u>; and yet these are the tokens of my daughter's virginity. And they shall spread the cloth before the elders of the city. And the elders of that city shall take that man and chastise him; And they shall amerce him in an hundred shekels of silver, and give them unto the father of the damsel, because he hath brought up an evil name upon a virgin of Israel: and she shall be his wife; he may not put her away all his days. But if this thing be true, and the tokens of virginity be not found for the damsel: Then they shall bring out the damsel to the door of her father's house, and the men of her city shall stone her with stones that she die: because she hath wrought folly in Israel, to play the whore in her father's house: so shalt thou put evil away from among you,* Deut 22:13-21**

In that text, God gave a law that dealt with the scenario of a man who had just married a young virgin woman and then accused her of not being pure when she actually was. The proof of her sexual purity was to be found in the tokens of virginity which she was supposed to present to her parents as proof that she had remained virtuous. The tokens of virginity and first intercourse were a bloodstained bed sheet or article of clothing, which was stained by blood from her broken hymen, which should have only been broken by her new husband on their wedding night.[51]

When the proof was presented, the husband who so recklessly slandered his new wife despite taking her virginity on their wedding night was fined 100 shekels of silver which would be given to her father, and then for an added penalty, he could never lawfully divorce her for any reason at all. What we can learn from that passage is how important the virginity of a young girl is to God. Think about it. If every unmarried girl would resolutely remain a virgin, especially because the law of God required it, that would also force unmarried young males to be chaste too. Now another point about this passage is that it used the term damsel which means young girl. It was not uncommon for brides of that day to be as young as ten years old.[52]

The scripture shows how important it was for the girl who married to be virtuous. Since they married at very young ages, it is evident that it was possible for a girl that young or younger to have already lost her virginity as it is today. If the new bride was not virtuous, which would have been based on the lack of the proof of virginity to present to her parents after her wedding night, that is, the lack of a blood stained article, she could have been stoned to death.

Now that may sound very harsh to a reader not familiar with the particulars of the Torah that was given to Israel. The first thing that must be understood is that this law was given by God Himself, and was not a concoction of Moses. So why does God sound so harsh? Actually He is not harsh, but instead has a much higher expectation of us than we may have of ourselves. Here, God is showing a female that her virginity is as precious as her life and that He wants her to guard it closely. In the days of the Old Testament, failure to guard her virginity was also failure to guard her life. Not only that, her unwillingness to guard her virginity is done at the expense of the corruption of males, and the destruction of morals. God's desire is that her virtue be given only to her husband, the man responsible to care for her for the rest of his life. God placed a value upon the female that He wanted her to place upon herself. He does not want her to be used, abused, or thrown away, but loved, cherished and kept. God did not want wanton promiscuity in Israel. Remember, there would have been very young pre-teen and teen girls giving up their virginity otherwise! The phrase "wrought folly in Israel" meant that she had acted foolishly because she had promiscuously given up her virginity. Now in all honesty, who can argue with that? When a woman or girl engages in premarital sex, she puts herself at risk for various complications including disease, pregnancy, complications of pregnancy, childbirth, complications from childbirth, permanent health problems, and even death. Why would a woman or a young girl want to put herself at risk for a male who only wants to enjoy sexual pleasure at her expense for a few minutes and make no investment into her life whatsoever? God also considers her loss of virginity in a non-marital relationship evil, and in our day His judgment has not changed, even though a female's life is no longer immediately be required of her. What about the man? Apparently God has given the sole responsibility of protecting virginity to the female. After all, it did belong to her, and she had to guard it with her life and not frivolously give it away, because it was her life.

Suppose that the charges made against the new wife were true. The precept in verse 21 determined that she was guilty because she had "played the whore" in Israel and sinned against God and herself by not remaining virtuous while unmarried. The lesson that can be learned here is that it did not matter whether she had sex only once, or a thousand times or received pay for it or not. When she lost her virginity, she became a whore by God's judgment. Since God has not, and does not change His judgments, in His eyes the girl or woman today who willfully engages in sex with anyone who is not her husband is considered by Him to be a whore.

Adultery

The next lesson taught in Deuteronomy 22 is that of adultery. The text says:

If a man be found lying with a woman married to an husband, then they shall both of them die, both the man that lay with the woman, and the woman: so shalt thou put away evil from Israel. Deuteronomy 22:22

Adultery was also a capital offense, punishable by death. We can see that God placed the same condemnation upon a woman who lost her virginity before marriage and disappointed her newlywed husband as that placed upon a woman who committed adultery. They were considered equally evil and the penalty for either act was the same.

Adultery is also used in the scriptures to symbolize idolatry because unfaithfulness to God is equivalent to unfaithfulness to a husband. The analogy is used many times to depict how Israel ended up abandoning the God who was a husband to them and who brought them out of Egypt to their independence in the land of promise and worshipping the gods of the Canaanites and idols that were crafted by their own skills in a spiritual act of adultery.[53]

Rape

Now let's move to the next lesson. The scripture reads:

If a damsel that is a virgin be betrothed unto an husband, and a man find her in the city, and lie with her; Then ye shall bring them both out unto the gate of that city, and ye shall stone them with stones that they die; the damsel, because she cried not, being in the city and the man, because he hath humbled his neighbour's wife: so thou shalt put away evil from among you. Deut 22:23-24

Considering the natural submissive nature of females, or the natural tendency of females to sometimes be weaker physically than males, especially those who are still somewhat young, adolescent, and naive, it is easy to see how a man could find her, and then perhaps seduce or strong-arm her into sexual intercourse. Either way, we call that rape. However, as we said before, God has higher expectations of all people, thus His greater valuation of a girl's virginity. So in this law, He stipulated that a female should at the very least cry out for her virginity, especially if this assault occurred within the city limits where people were numerically present and were in earshot of her cries. God expected a woman or a girl to scream and resist and not allow a man to easily rob her of the precious gift of virginity that He had given to her, and more so if she was betrothed to another man. At the time of this writing, there was an incident of a 12 year old girl who was forcefully taken by a man and shoved into his truck. This girl however, fought and screamed and hit him repeatedly, giving him such a hard time that the attacker put her out and drove off. Imagine a day when it was impossible to abduct a girl and drive off quickly. Add to that, the idea of a girl being in an area full of city people with no glass windows or sealed building structures that could seal out silence. A girl could receive help quickly by screaming and the perpetrator would be caught quickly. God knew that and wanted to see Israelite females fight for their virginity which could be easily protected by such resistance. He wanted them to struggle against any perpetration against their purity, dignity, and possibly their lives.

Betrothal was equal to marriage itself and required divorce measures to dissolve it. The biblical account of Mary and Joseph that describes the circumstances of the Messiah's birth bears that fact out.[54] Joseph could have had Mary stoned on the basis of the Deuteronomy 22:23-24 passage, but he chose not to. Instead, he chose to break off the relationship secretly, i.e. "divorce" her without making a big deal of it. On that issue Adam Clarke stated that despite the fact that the marriage had not been consummated, their relationship was legal and binding and could not be broken except by divorce.[55] The archangel Gabriel convinced Joseph not to divorce her because her pregnancy was not the result of a breach of the betrothal, but rather by a sovereign act of God.

So if it was discovered that a betrothed girl was forced into losing her virginity in a place where her cries for help could be heard and she failed to cry out, she would have been put to death along with the male who forced her. Now the rest of the lesson goes like this:

> *But if a man find a betrothed damsel in the field, and the man force her, and lie with her: then the man only that lay with her shall die: But unto the damsel thou shalt do nothing, there is in the damsel no sin worthy of death: for as when a man riseth against his neighbour, and slayeth him, even so is this matter: For he found her in the field and the betrothed damsel cried, and there was none to save her.*
> Deut 22:25-27

If she was accosted in a remote area where her cries for help would have been in vain, only then would she have been guiltless where the loss of her virginity was concerned. He cries would not have been able to save her. This edict that came from the mind and mouth of God is really saying, "Don't let a man take your virginity from you if you can help it. Fight for your virtue and cry out for help." Is that not similar to the message of the people today who encourage women and girls not to allow males to take advantage of them? Do we not teach our children to say "No!" when someone touches them in a sexual way and then to tell someone as quickly as possible? As we get to know God better, we begin to understand the wisdom behind His precepts, and they begin to make more sense, although they may not make much sense initially. The main lesson that you should get from these passages is the value that God places on virginity when a female is not married.

Now for the next lesson that Deuteronomy 22 teaches. We read:

> *If a man find a damsel that is a virgin, which is not betrothed, and lay hold on her, and lie with her, and they be found; Then the man that lay with her shall give unto the damsel's father fifty shekels of silver, and she shall be his wife; because he hath humbled her, he may not put her away all his days.*
> Deut 22:28-29

We have here the same kind of situation as the last except neither is married. A man accosts a girl in Israel and wantonly seduces her sexually. The factor of crying out for help is not mentioned. If caught, he must marry her. The man who forced her would have to pay her father a dowry of fifty shekels of silver, and he would never be able to divorce her. Remembering the first lesson taught about a girl who married but was not found to be a virgin, this arrangement would be in her best interest, especially since she allowed him to take her virginity without resistance. Her failure to resist him and then be quiet about it would work against her later on if she married but was not found to be a virgin. If her new husband was upset enough about her impurity, he could have her put to death. Therefore, a female really needed to put up a good struggle to keep her virtue and not allow it to be easily taken from her.

Here is another thing to keep in mind. As an Israelite, she was to be taught the law of God, as well as her brothers. Therefore, she would know the ramifications of her failure to respond beforehand and the problems she could encounter later. Knowing what God required of her, that should have given her enough incentive for her to fight for herself. In all honesty, God's law, teaching her to fight to keep her virginity is much better than the weakness exhibited by females today who willingly and easily give up their virtue as though it is worth nothing, and many times to individuals who have no intention of engaging in a lasting, loving, and committed relationship anyway, or who have no good character at all.

Such laws are in keeping with the idea that God made the woman for the man. Yet, God did not want men to use women and then throw them away. God puts sex on the same level with marriage and commitment and it is highly prized in His eyes. Consider the many men and women who are willingly sexual with each other without any consideration of a life-long commitment. Based on the Torah, those who do so violate His law and they must give an account for their sin. The only escape from God's judgment is total repentance and turning to Jesus the Messiah who is the only one who can atone for such sins against the practical commandments of God.

Here is another point to consider. God's laws are not like our laws. In today's society, it is possible that someone may violate a law and not realize it, but be called to account for it later on despite his lack of knowing that he had violated a law. God's laws were not designed to be like that. Children were supposed to be taught God's laws every day as soon as they were able to understand. So the things presented here were not supposed to be unknown concepts that would suddenly become a surprise to them later. If they were surprised, they were not supposed to be, but they would have been if they were not taught the laws of God, or had forgotten them. They were supposed to know those commands in early childhood to keep from violating them.

Now you may wonder what ever happens to the man who had sex with a virgin girl, never married her, and became the cause of her possibly losing her life when she could later show no tokens of her virginity. Does he get away? Not really. God sees all, and knows all. That man would himself also be judged by the law of God for his violation. Remember, the law of God said that he was supposed to marry her and not leave her in jeopardy. His failure to marry her would have also been sin. Though he may not have been judged immediately, he would not have been guiltless before God.

From the New Testament, we can add to the lesson with the following verse of scripture:

Marriage is to be held in honor among all, and the marriage bed is to be undefiled; for fornicators and adulterers God will judge. Hebrews 13:4 NASU

If that's what God requires, He did not begin requiring that in Jesus' day because that has always been His intent, and the New Testament bears that out. God's challenge was to teach us so that we could know and understand what He wants. The man who has sex with a woman and never marries her has sinned against God and is in danger of God's judgment.

Various Other Laws Governing Sexual Behavior

In Deuteronomy 12:1, God told Moses to tell the sons of Israel that they were to live according to the statutes that He had commanded them to live by for the rest of their lives. The sons of Israel were responsible to bring those laws to the hearing of all of the people. Moses would transmit God's words to the elders, and then the elders would transmit God's words to the leaders of groups of families, who would transmit those words to the family heads, who would transmit His words to the heads of the households, who would teach their individual families the commands of God. God's ultimate plan was to teach all of Israel so that they could be an example of and teach the rest of the world His laws, precepts, statutes, and judgments. In this segment, several laws concerning sexual behavior are shown and a number of rather explicit sexual acts are listed in Leviticus chapter 18. One very important fact to note here is that all of the commandments listed in this section identify unrighteous sexual behavior, regardless of the reason or circumstances. They are:

Incest

1) **Verse 6:** The men of Israel were not to approach anyone who was closely related to them for sexual pleasure. Apparently, this was the practice of the Canaanites. The vast difference between this and the incestuous marriages that were common earlier is that at the time, the marriages were necessary for human and family development, lifelong commitment and procreation rather than momentary sexual gratification. The Canaanites had degenerated to where men were using every female in the family only

for their own sexual gratification. God wanted to unfold his perfect and holy guidelines for His creation, and clean up Canaan to put a stop to the degeneration. Israel would be the instrument that God would use for that purpose. He would also use the nation to put His name in the land of Israel geographically as a holy place of worship and a central place for the rest of the world to learn about, worship, and understand the God of creation. Females had spread out into the world far enough so that incestuous marriages had become unnecessary. The goal was to prevent females from being used simply for a man's momentary sexual pleasure.

2) **Verse 7:** A son was not to approach his mother for sex. The phrase "father's nakedness" meant that his mother's body was a privilege reserved only for his father to enjoy alone.

3) **Verse 8:** A man was forbidden to approach his step-mother for sex.

4) **Verse 9:** A man was forbidden to approach his sister, half-sister, or step-sister for sex, regardless of who she lived with.

5) **Verse 10:** A man was forbidden to approach his granddaughter for sex.

6) **Verse 11:** A man was forbidden to approach his step-sister for sex. In God's eyes she is as a blood relative.

7) **Verses 12-13**: A man was forbidden to approach his blood related aunts for sex.

8) **Verses 14:** It was forbidden for a man to approach his step-aunt, that is, his uncle's wife

(not blood-related) for sex. Note that she is considered to be the uncle's "nakedness."

9) **Verse 15:** It was forbidden for a man to approach his daughter-in-law for sex.

10) **Verse 16:** It was forbidden for a man to approach his sister-in-law for sex. Again, her "nakedness" is said to belong to his brother.

11) **Verse 17:** It was forbidden for a man to be sexual with both a woman and her daughter(s) or her granddaughter(s). Although it was lawful for a man to have two wives, those wives could not be both a mother and her daughter.[56]

12) **Verse 18:** It was forbidden for a man to marry both a woman and her sister. Here again is a reference to polygamy in the law of God.

Homosexual Sex

13) **Verse 22:** It was forbidden for a man to have sex with another man. The obvious implication here is that sexual pleasure is to be given to a man by a woman, specifically a wife, and not another man. This is confirmation of the truth that was stated in a previous chapter that "whenever and whereever same-sex sex is mention in scripture, it is repudiated and condemned." The penalty for such was death which helps us to see God's perspective of this behavior.

Bestiality

14) **Verse 23:** It was forbidden for a man (or a woman) to have sexual intercourse with an animal.

The preceding verses covered a range of what was sexually prohibited by God. A very important point to see here is that these are practical laws, the ones that govern our behavior for which we are responsible. Jesus' death on the cross did not abrogate any of these in any way.

Penalties

The 20th chapter of Leviticus covers punishment for sexual sins under the law. Since these precepts came from God Himself, we can get a picture of how He feels about them when they are committed, regardless of what others' opinions about them may be. Moses did not make any of these up. He received all of these statutes directly from God during his extended stay in the presence of God while on Mount Sinai.[57] God gave them to identify what sin is, how horrible it is in His eyes and how He intended to punish those who committed them. Let's take a look at each one:

1) **Verse 10:** The penalty for adultery was death for both the man and the woman who committed it. Adultery is the act of a married person having

sexual intercourse with someone else who is not that person's spouse.

2) **Verse 11:** If a man had sex with his step-mother, both he and his step-mother could be executed.

3) **Verse 12:** If a man had sex with his daughter-in-law, both he and his daughter-in-law could be executed, and they alone would be responsible for their deaths.

4) **Verse 13:** If a man had sex with another man, both of them would be executed. God considers such an act as detestable, and the two of them would be solely responsible for the fact that they were put to death. God did not consider it cruel or unusual that they would be civilly executed for such an act.

5) **Verse 14:** The man who married a woman and her daughter would have been *burned with fire* along with the daughter and her mother. To God, that was a heinous sin worthy of death for all of them.

6) **Verses 15-16:** The man or woman who had sex with an animal was to be executed. The poor animal that had no part in the decision to commit the original offense was to be killed as well for being sexually defiled by a human being.

7) **Verse 17:** The man who had sex with his sister was to be executed along with his sister. The expression 'cut off' is another expression for being put to death (see I Kings 18:4).

8) **Verse 18:** The man who had sex with a menstruating woman (not his wife) was to be cut off' as well along with the woman.

9) **Verse 19-20:** The man who had sex with his aunt would die along with the aunt. The phrase "they shall bear their sin" means that they would be solely responsible for the consequences of their actions.

10) **Verse 21:** If a man had sex with his sister-in-law, he too would be sentenced to death. The usual method was by stoning (see verses 2 & 27) unless otherwise noted. The phrase they shall die childless probably means that even if she had gotten pregnant, she would probably still be executed.

What about Laws against Lesbianism?

An interesting omission: there is no specific law given to God by Moses that prohibited a woman from having sex with another woman. A law specifically prohibited a man from having sex with a man but there was none given where women were concerned. Why? Remember that earlier we established that God made the woman for the man:

For the man is not of the woman; but the woman of the man. Neither was the man created for the woman; but the woman for the man. 1 Corinthians 11:8-9

The woman was made for the man and given as a gift to man. Paul does not say that a man was made for a man, or that a woman was made for a woman. A woman is a special gift from God, made biologically compatible and therefore naturally complementary for a man. If the woman was made for the man, then we can use this common term to sum it up: "That's a wrap!" The woman was the one given in marriage to the man. So then if she acted otherwise sexually, her behavior is in defiance to the will of God, and a denial of His purpose and of how and what He created her for. In addition, a close look at both Leviticus 18:22 and Leviticus 20:13 reveals a woman's purpose for the man. Both passages prohibit men from acting in the sexual role that only a woman was specifically designed for. Therefore, one can see God's intent for the woman from those passages alone.

The list of sexual prohibitions was compiled so that one could see all sexual sin from God's perspective. There is so much talk against homosexuality today in Christian circles until many people may forget that there are other sexual sins that also bring God's judgment such as heterosexual fornication and heterosexual adultery. When those sins are committed, the violators are in just as much trouble with God as are those who are inclined towards same-sex sex. The contention they are committed in "love" is not enough to prevent God's punishment.

Two More Points
Judging

First of all, the penalties for these offences were to be executed by men. What kind of men could execute this kind of judgment? Only men who were free themselves from these sins. Jesus taught that when a person judged, he would be judged (by God) by the same standard of judgment with which he judged.[58] So if the person or persons rendering the sentence were themselves not guilty of sin, they would have nothing to worry about. If not, then they too would be in danger of God's judgment which is probably why the accusers of the woman who was caught in the act of adultery in the account of John 8 and brought to Jesus in question of His judgment, left instead of stoning her. He had said that whoever was without sin should be the first to cast a stone at her. Apparently, none of her accusers were guiltless, and were therefore unable to judge her worthy of condemnation by stoning.

Many people are deceived about "judging" and they will contend that we should not "judge" anyone. But that is not possible for we are always judging and making judgments and that is inescapable. Judging is simply *making a decision*. We must make decisions and determine whether something is right or wrong before we do it. God's word helps us to make proper judgments and decisions. For example, God said, "You shall not steal." We know that stealing is taking possession of something that rightfully belongs to someone else. When God said, don't steal, God had judged that act of taking something belonging to someone else as a wrongful act. I, on the other hand, have judged, or made a decision to agree with God's decree that it is wrong to steal. Since God has already declared that a sexual act between two men is disgusting (abominable) in His sight, if any two men behave sexually towards each other, I can say they are wrong because God has already established and decided that it is wrong. My decision not to do that is based on God's decision already laid down. If I in fact believe Him and his judgments (decisions), then I will obey Him and accept and agree with his judgments. Thus, the original decision (judgment) on the subject is not mine, but God's. So in this matter when you tell me not to judge, you are actually demanding that I should not decide to agree with God and His judgment. Besides – when you accuse me of judging as if I am doing something wrong, you are judging me!

Marriages God Will Recognize

The second point is a little more challenging for some, but truthful. God will not condemn the sexual relations between an adolescent girl who is legally married to a male regardless of his age, or the marriage of an adolescent boy who is legally married to a woman regardless of age, or the marriage of more than one woman with one man. But He will never ever validate same-sex sexual relationships because He has never done so, based on what we have seen from the bible so far. The reason is that the only Godly justification for intercourse has always been male/female marriage. Now I am not by any means advocating or promoting the marriage of persons under the legal age of majority, nor am I promoting polygamy. I am simply saying that where that is the accepted custom, God will not frown upon sexual intercourse between a husband and his wife whether that wife is a girl or a woman, or that husband is a boy or man, because God has already validated those relationships before, and He will continue to validate them as long as they continue to occur. But He will not ever validate any gay relationships under any circumstances. We can see from the aforementioned texts that God's plan and intent for male and female sexual relationships is that sexual intercourse take place only in marriage between a male and a female and not in promiscuous, indiscriminate, and wanton sexual behavior outside of that relationship.

Chapter Five

A BETTER UNDERSTANDING OF THE TORAH AND ITS PURPOSE

*here are many things about the Torah that our enlightened and complex modern minds will have difficulty with because it involved an ancient Jewish culture that God used to teach His standards to all cultures, including ours. Thus, the information in the previous chapter could well have produced questions. In light of that possibility, this chapter will attempt to help readers better understand the nature and intent of the Torah. God intended for the righteousness of His laws to transcend all time, people, and cultures. If anyone does not believe that is possible, then their best perception of God is that He is flawed and limited. I do not believe that anyone who acknowledges God really intends to make that kind of *judgment* (there's that word again!) against Him.

Now in order to understand the Torah better, we must go back to when the Torah was introduced. So for a moment, let's forget about our times, our culture, and look at the Hebrew people living in Egypt under slavery as described in the book of Exodus.

The Hebrew people were working extra hard under the demanding harshness of the Egyptian taskmasters, who at the command of Pharoah would motivate the Jewish foremen chosen by Egyptian overseers to drive the forced labor even harder by beating and abusing them when the quotas of bricks were not met even though the Egyptians had stopped providing the raw materials.[59] That's because Moses, the Hebrew who was raised in Egypt, had met with his people in obedience to the command of God, and told them that God was going to release them from slavery. But they had no idea that God was going to harden Pharaoh's heart first so that he would be stubborn and not release them immediately. Instead, Pharaoh gave the Hebrew people a very hard time.[60] The Egyptian King made slavery even more difficult for Israel. But this had been done so that God could demonstrate His power[61] to Israel in an effort to build faith in them for their God, and to help them to understand that their manumission was more than the work of Moses alone.[62]

God demonstrated his power through 10 miraculous plagues that delivered Israel but created extreme hardship and sorrow for the Egyptians. The last plague killed all of the firstborn of animals and people of the Egyptians.[63] Reluctantly, Pharaoh released them, only to hotly pursue them in what would be a futile effort to force them back because the pursuers all drowned in the Red Sea.[64] The Israelites saw God's power and should have concluded that their release was not due to the diplomatic expertise of Moses, but rather to the God of their fathers—Abraham, Isaac, and Jacob, who had met Moses at the miraculous sight of a bush that was on fire, but was not actually burning.[65]

The burning bush, the plagues, the other miracles, the signs, and the parting of the Red Sea were all important precursors to the giving of the Torah, which would become the civil law manual of the Hebrew people. So as we read and study, if we fail to see the intent of God behind the commandments, then we must ask God to reveal to us His intent so that we might ascertain the truth of His motivation as He gave, by His estimation, the highest form of law and governance ever given to man. As stated in chapter 1, this is what He has said about Himself as it regards His principles that come from His mind:

For my thoughts are not your thoughts, neither are your ways my ways, saith the LORD. For as the heavens are higher than the earth, so are my ways higher than your ways, and my thoughts than your thoughts. Isaiah 55:8-9

God declared that His concepts are higher and better than ours. Anyone wishing to argue with the Creator of heaven and earth may be my guest. I however, find it difficult to argue with someone who has created the universe with all of its resources and potential.

For who hath known the mind of the Lord, that he may instruct him? 1 Corinthians 2:16

Since I do not have the power to teach or advise God, I will simply believe Him rather than argue with Him and then ask Him to help me to understand what I don't understand.

Now going back to the point just made: all the commandments came from God, and they reflect the highest standard of living for man which is righteousness. They were given to a fledgling nation that had experienced slavery and oppression before gaining their independence from Egypt. The nation would now be governed by a new standard given to them by their God after reaching the Promised land. So for Israel at this time, all of the laws were new and neither the purpose nor the intent of the laws, nor their responsibility to God with respect to the laws were fully understood by the newly birthed nation.

The Intent of the Sex Laws

Now imagine God giving these laws to the Hebrew people for the first time. Moses was the agent who brought them to the citizens of this new nation. Would there be any objection to any of the laws? Would there be any questions? No, not immediately. Questions would certainly come, and desire to understand purpose and intent would also become an issue, as with any legislation. But this new nation was in no position to question any of it at this time. Now imagine the laws governing what appeared to be forced sex in some cases, such as that which we read in the previous chapter and it's consequence — a dowry payment to the girl's father and marriage without the benefit of divorce, or death when she failed to cry out for help if she is forced into sex while engaged to someone else. Whereas our western minds may have trouble comprehending such consequences, yet there is merit that can be realized when you step back and see the entire picture.

First of all there is a specific directive that God had given to Israel that was imperative to the spiritual survival of the nation which said:

Therefore shall ye lay up these my words in your heart and in your soul, and bind them for a sign upon your hand, that they may be as frontlets between your eyes. And ye shall teach them [to] your children, speaking of them when thou sittest in thine house, and when thou walkest by the way, when thou liest down, and when thou risest up. And thou shalt write them upon the door posts of thine house, and upon thy gates: That your days may be multiplied, and the days of your children, in the land which the LORD sware unto your fathers to give them, as the days of heaven upon the earth.
Deuteronomy 11:18-21*

If Israel would obey this one directive, it would guaranteed the nation's survival and God's protection, provision, and intervention on their behalf. We can see that God wanted His people to obsess themselves with His laws and precepts, and talk about them all the time around the home in the hearing of their children.

Imagine a very young boy of about four or five years old who begins to hear of God's laws as his father teaches them to him on a constant basis, revealing the deadly consequences of having sex with a married or betrothed girl, or knowing that if he persuades an unattached girl to have sex with him, he must marry her after paying the father a dowry and be unable to divorce her ever. What if he hears that over and over again until he reaches puberty? Certainly those precepts would have had an influencing effect on a young mind that was steered to respect his God and his father's teachings of the laws God. God's intent was that his father influence the boy to understand that sex was not to be taken frivolously, but experienced in marriage only. If it happened before marriage, then it should necessitate a marriage.

God did not want Israelite girls and women to be whores by promiscuity, or misused by selfish opportunists either. They would learn that marriage would prevent the whore label (by God) and keep the sexual aspect of the union pure. A young man could end up marrying more than one girl or woman, but he would know that he had to marry them before engaging sexually with them, or he could be executed. He would also learn that God considered divorce an act of hard-heartedness. Thus, the boy would learn that God hated divorce.[66]

The boy was also taught about the consequences of all sexual behavior that God declared to be sin, such as the possibility of execution if a man were caught having sex with another man or with an animal for example, because both acts are disgusting in the sight of God. While God's intent was to influence His people with His laws, Israel's problem (as well as ours) was that they failed to do all the things that God's laws instructed them to do.

Then the father would turn his attention to his daughter and teach her that it is imperative that she maintain her virginity at all costs, even if attacked. We tell girls today to speak up and to say "No!"; to scream; and to tell someone. The teaching was actually promoting the same principle with a slightly different twist that could be effective in the prevention of forced sex. The girl would have learned the danger of giving up her virginity and possibly have been inspired to do everything she could to keep it. The main point of the command was to teach us about how God views sex. To the male, God says that if she is good enough for you to have sex with, then she is good enough for you to marry and keep for a lifetime. Therefore a boy growing up in Israel who was taught the law of God knew that if he forced an unmarried female sexually, she could become his wife forever; or that if he engaged in sexual intercourse with a betrothed or married female, he could be executed. A girl would be taught that God said that if you don't stop him, then he must marry you, else he may ruin or cause you to lose your life, or you could become his wife forever. Such teachings from The Almighty would empower and encourage a female to maintain her virtue.

There is a biblical incident that occurred that had similarities to that kind of situation long before this law was given. But before I show that incident, I will point out that it is evident that marriage occurred under quite different circumstances than it occurs now. Generally in modern times, a man will ask the female to marry him, and in most cases in the Western world and in some of the rest of the world the decision to do so is strictly up to her. The customs of ancient Israel in the days preceding the giving of the law were different. The father tended to be in charge of his daughter's marriage, or if the woman was a slave, then her owner was in charge of whether or not she married, and to whom. Her owner may have even decided to maintain her as a servant wife for himself and if that were the case, she became his *concubine*.[67] As a concubine she served him menially, and he provided food and shelter for her. Her status was still that of a slave, but also of a wife for conjugal purposes.[68]

Women accepted those conditions as the norm and as what was expected of them. They were given in marriage either by previous arrangement by their fathers, by an impulsive decision by the father, or sometimes a male would see a girl and immediately desire her for a wife. In such a case, that male may ask his own father to negotiate with her family about that possibility, or he might be able to make his own arrangements with her father to procure her as a wife.[69] If there was an agreement, then the male would be willing to give whatever dowry was required of him. The dowry, which was a gift to the family—or as some believe to the bride[70]—proved a man's personal wealth and strength, and his ability to care for his wife and eventual family.

Because those women accepted those customs, some people today may think that their reticence was awful. The following biblical incident somewhat fits right in with the Torah law on its response to forced sex and marriage.

Forced Sex and Marriage

Now this situation took place long before Israel received the Torah from God. As a matter of fact, it transpired long before Israel's slavery. In Genesis 34 we have the story of Dinah, the son of Jacob and his wife Leah. Dinah may have probably been as young as 13 years old when this event occurred.[71] Her family had settled in the city of Shalem. Dinah, being the only girl in a family of 12 boys, had ventured out to associate with her friends. Along the way, she was spotted by Shechem, who was the son of Hamor, the Chief of the city. When Shechem, being the prince of the ruling family saw Dinah, he was immediately attracted to her, and forced her to have sexual intercourse with him. His approach was without a doubt inappropriate by any standards. But despite his crude introduction to Dinah, he professed his love for her and wanted her to become his wife. Dinah's age and perhaps Shechem's royal personage and authority probably explains her passive lack of resistance to his advances. Not surprisingly, her brothers were enraged, and knowing that they were at a disadvantage, used deception in order to gain revenge. Instead of a dowry, they required circumcision of every male in the city of Shalem which was just a ruse. The supposed agreement was that when the men of Shalem would be circumcised, then Jacob's family would be free to intermarry with any family in Shalem. However, when the men of Shalem were circumcised, sore, and scarcely able to walk, Jacob's sons moved in and slaughtered them all. Jacob was not pleased with what his sons had done because he realized that the people of the region would now distrust and hate them because of the extreme measure in which vengeance was taken. However, his sons stubbornly justified their actions by saying that Hamor should not have humbled their sister in the way that he did.[72]

The point is that Hamor, though he had indeed raped Dinah, was prepared to make amends through marriage which is the same principle of the law that God presented to Israel. Sadly, the overreaction of Jacob's sons was not warranted. It appears that if Jacob had agreed to the arrangement, Dinah would have simply complied. But Jacob's sons never allowed their father to make that decision. There is no purpose here to justify rape, but only to show the circumstantial similarity to God's law concerning forced sex and marriage, and the agreement that could have been reached between Jacob's sons and Hamar. We must remember that the main point of the forced sex precept was not so much to dwell on the consequences of the violation, but rather to teach avoidance of the behavior so that it would not be committed. This proves that God's ways are higher and infinitesimally better than ours.

Identifying Sin

The main point of the Laws of God was to teach man what sin is and teach him how to avoid it. The following verses of scripture bear that out plainly. Remember, what God has commanded must be obeyed. Here is what God said about Israel and Judah with respect to His laws,

But this thing commanded I them, saying, Obey my voice, and I will be your God, and ye shall be my people: and walk ye in all the ways that I have commanded you, that it may be well unto you. But they hearkened not, nor inclined their ear, but walked in the counsels and in the imagination of their evil heart, and went backward, and not forward. Since the day that your fathers came forth out of the land of Egypt unto this day I have even sent unto you all my servants the prophets, daily rising up early and sending them: Yet they hearkened not unto me, nor inclined their ear, but hardened their neck: they did worse than their fathers. Jeremiah 7:23-26

Israel disobeyed the commands that God gave them despite the fact that prophets were sent to warn them in an effort to persuade them to be obedient. But they stubbornly continued to be disobedient. Stubborn disobedience to God leads to deterioration and corruption in everything.

There is Nothing Unrighteous about the Torah

The apostle Paul taught that there is nothing unrighteous about the law of God. He declared that the law is not at fault, but man is because even though he hears the law of God, he violates it anyway. Scripture teaches that man is naturally prone to violate God's law because he is already naturally attracted to the sinful behavior that God condemns. Paul taught,

What shall we say then? Is the law sin? God forbid. Nay, I had not known sin, but by the law: for I had not known lust, except the law had said, Thou shalt not covet. Romans 7:7

Whosoever committeth sin transgresseth also the law: for sin is the transgression of the law. 1 John 3:4

In these two passages Paul revealed what sin is. The apostle Paul taught that if we violate the precepts of the Torah, we sin. The Torah identified sin for us and it is incumbent upon us to learn what sin is and then avoid it. Avoidance of sin is obeying God. Since Israel did not obey God, they paid the price. When we disobey God, we sin too, and will likewise pay a price. Only through repentance do we avoid that price. Additionally, Paul also taught that we already had an inclination to do things that would displease God even before the Torah identified them as sin. We do not learn that those actions are sins against God until after God's word has revealed that fact to us.

How the Torah was Transmitted

Now let's look at the commandments as they were being given to the children of Israel for the first time. Moses, the man appointed by God to be Israel's leader, had leadership ability, but what fledgeling Israel lacked was organization. He naively attempted to do the huge job of administration, counseling, adjudicating, and leadership alone, simply because he did not fully understand the depth of the responsibilities that he had, nor how difficult all that responsibility would be without help. So the following is what happened:

And it came to pass on the morrow, that Moses sat to judge the people: and the people stood by Moses from the morning unto the evening. Exodus 18:13

Moses did that every day, all day. It was a disaster waiting to happen that would eventually burn Moses out, and perhaps cause him to have a nervous breakdown. If that happened, Israel would be without a leader. Moses' actions also frustrated the people, too. Imagine being at the end of the line the previous day, and then waiting all day to see Moses, only to have him come out at the end of that long day saying that he was tired and couldn't see any more people so come back tomorrow. That must have been real fun! Also imagine that you returned a little later than you wanted the next day after standing in line all day the previous day and perhaps have another long wait. Since "taking a number" had probably not been thought of yet, it is obvious that this novice government by Moses was not going well at its inception.

But Jethro, Moses' father-in-law, had a great idea. He watched him and probably even heard rumblings among the people about how frustrating it was to get an audience with Moses. So one day, he pulled Moses on the side and asked him:

> "... *What is this thing that thou doest to the people? why sittest thou thyself alone, and all the people stand by thee from morning unto even?"* Exodus 18:14

Because Moses was Israel's leader, and he would receive answers from God based on His laws, he answered,

> "... *Because the people come unto me to inquire of God: When they have a matter, they come unto me; and I judge between one and another, and I do make them know the statutes of God, and his laws."* Exodus 18:15-16

Jethro proceeded to show Moses what his mistake was, and then gave him a better solution that required some training and organization. He said:

". . . The thing that thou doest is not good. Thou wilt surely wear away, both thou, and this people that is with thee: for this thing is too heavy for thee; thou art not able to perform it thyself alone. Hearken now unto my voice, I will give thee counsel, and God shall be with thee: Be thou for the people to Godward, that thou mayest bring the causes unto God: And thou shalt teach them ordinances and laws, and shalt shew them the way wherein they must walk, and the work that they must do. Moreover thou shalt provide out of all the people able men, such as fear God, men of truth, hating covetousness; and place such over them, to be rulers of thousands, and rulers of hundreds, rulers of fifties, and rulers of tens: And let them judge the people at all seasons: and it shall be, that every great matter they shall bring unto thee, but every small matter they shall judge: so shall it be easier for thyself, and they shall bear the burden with thee. If thou shalt do this thing, and God command thee so, then thou shalt be able to endure, and all this people shall also go to their place in peace. Exodus 18:17-23

Moses took the advice of his father-in-law and set up the leadership of the nation using that structure. The people chosen in these leadership roles of the nation were men only. Women were to be submissive—not subservient. They were responsible for the children and matters at home, and men were responsible for the overall care, protection, feeding, sheltering, and general upkeep of their families, and selected men were responsible for the governance and order of the nation.

The Torah Recognized Men as Leaders

Now the concept of men being leaders is very important to the way the Torah was received. Moses had set up a definite hierarchal structure of leadership with seventy elders who reported directly to him. Following the advice of his father-in-law, these men would have been responsible for thousands of leaders under them. Those thousands would have been broken up into groups of hundreds and the hundreds were broken up into groups of ten. Each group had leaders who were upwards responsible to the elders and ultimately to Moses. God used this structure to further assist Moses for the work that he would do because in the next chapter, God said to Moses,

> ' *These are the words that you shall speak to the sons of Israel.*" Ex 19:6 NASU

Then,

> *. . . Moses came and called for the elders of the people, and laid before their faces all these words which the LORD commanded him*. Exodus 19:7

Moses told the elders, the elders relayed the messages to the leaders of thousands, they in turn relayed the messages to their respective subordinates until all of the people got the messages. After receiving the messages the people responded,

> *". . . All that the LORD hath spoken we will do"*. Exodus 19:8

The point being made is this: the commandments were always given to and through the *men* of Israel by God. Thus, everything written has a masculine ring to it. Not understanding this structure, the bible, or its message, feminists have been dismayed by that fact and as a result have accused the bible of being "chauvinist." But that is the way God chose to transmit his word. Again, I will not argue with the Sovereign. So when you read the commandments, you are reading what was given by God to *men* and through *men* to all of the people.

Men led, protected, and made decisions for their families and the nation. In keeping with the precedent set by God, they tried made sure that their daughters got good husbands and providers for them and their potential families. At the time, men were in complete charge, and women were submissive, evidenced by the way that the law was written. The woman was first submissive to her father growing up as a little girl, and then as a grown woman she was given by her father to a husband to whom she would be submissive. Women had little say in the establishment of marital relationships and it was expected that a woman would be given in marriage to a man, even as set by God's precedent

This chapter is designed to assist in the understanding of the Torah and to show how it influenced decisions and culture in Israel. Culture may change, but God did not intend for culture to shape His standards. He rather intended for His standards to shape culture. Culture not influenced by God's standards will eventually destroy people and whole civilizations.[73] We have difficulty relating to God's standards today only because we naturally have difficulty relating to God's righteousness. Israel had the same problem. What we learn from the bible is that regardless of time or culture, man's nature is the same. The bible is about man's nature and that nature is the nature of sin that does not want God's righteousness to bother it. To man's nature, God's standards are a nuisance. A part of us wants what is right, but we do not naturally want all of what is right the way that God wants us to experience it. We prefer it our way. Many of us will initially reject what God wants for us. Not only is that what the bible teaches, but it is confirmed by our actions. What makes us repent is that we finally come to our senses and sorrowfully realize that we have sinned against a God who loves us, causing us to come to Jesus for forgiveness and salvation. Only then can we become conpletely open to the truth of God. Prior to that, like the religious Saul of Tarsus, many of us will vehemently reject God and His standards. Here is the reason:

Because the carnal mind is enmity against God: for it is not subject to the law of God, neither indeed can be. Romans 8:7

Man struggles with sin because he wrestles against the righteousness of God.

Chapter Six

WHAT THE BIBLE TEACHES ABOUT HOMOSEXUALITY

*W*hat does the bible actually teach about homosexuality? The answer does not have to be contrived. The bible is explicit about what we call homosexuality and God's attitude towards it. As we have already seen, God is not even pleased with every male/female relationship that involves sex, or even marriage, although He may show mercy on some marriages, such as in King David's case. But a gay relationship cannot ever receive such mercy from God because it is totally unacceptable in nature from the beginning. Two facts are constant and undeniable throughout scripture. The first is, although homosexuality is not mentioned much in scripture, whenever it is mentioned, it is mentioned in a negative and repudiated context, and there are no exceptions.

The second is, whenever marriage is mentioned, it is always mentioned in the context of a relationship between a male and one or more females and there are no exceptions.

According to the Webster's Random House Dictionary, the word *homosexuality* is defined as "sexual desire or behavior directed toward a person or persons of one's own sex." The word was never used in early English translations of the bible because at the time they were written, the word did not exist. Instead, other words or phrases were used and always in repudiation of same-sex sex. *Homosexual* and *homosexuality* are relatively recent coinages that came into usage circa 1890-95. Their recent addition as words to the language does not justify nor preclude the sinfulness of such behavior for it does not matter how we label it. God has already condemned sexual acts of any kind between same-sex individuals as sin, modern labeling or even societal acceptance of such notwithstanding. The words and phrases used in the earlier English translations describe same-sex activity in such a way that is clear to the reader what is being discussed with very little research required. And there are stories in the bible where the desire for such acts is evident and the repudiation of the desire is also evident, thus demonstrating the attitude that God wants all of us to have towards homosexual behavior. The first of such instances is found in Genesis chapter 19. The entire context of scripture will be inserted here to bolster the point.

Sodom and Gomorrah

And there came two angels to Sodom <u>at even</u> [in the evening]*; and Lot sat in the gate of Sodom: and Lot seeing them rose up to meet them; and he bowed himself with his face toward the ground; And he said, Behold now, my lords, turn in, I <u>pray you</u>,* [ask] *into your servant's house, and tarry all night, and wash your feet, and ye shall rise up early, and go on your ways. And they said, Nay; but we will abide in the street all night. And he pressed upon them greatly; and they turned in unto him, and entered into his house; and he made them a feast, and did bake unleavened bread, and they did eat. But before they lay down, the men of the city, even the men of Sodom, compassed the house round, both old and young, all the people from every quarter: And they called unto Lot, and said unto him, Where are the men which came in to thee this night? bring them out unto us, that we <u>may know</u>* [have sex with] *them. And Lot went out at the door unto them, and shut the door after him, And said, I pray you, brethren, do not so wickedly. Behold now, I have two daughters <u>which have not known man</u>* [are virgins]*; let me, I pray you, bring them out unto you, <u>and do ye to them as is good in your eyes</u>* [have sex with them as much as you want]*: only unto these men do nothing; for therefore came they under the shadow of my roof And they*

125

said, Stand back And they said again This one fellow <u>came in to sojourn</u> [is a foreigner], *and he <u>will needs</u>* [wants to] *be a judge: now will we deal worse with thee, than with them. And they pressed sore upon the man, even Lot, and came near to break the door. But the men put forth their hand, and pulled Lot into the house to them, and shut to the door. And they <u>smote</u>* [struck] *the men that were at the door of the house with blindness, both small and great: so that they wearied themselves to find the door. And the men said unto Lot, Hast thou here any besides? son in law, and thy sons, and thy daughters, and whatsoever thou hast in the city, bring them out of this place: For we will destroy this place, because the <u>cry of</u>* [protest against] *them <u>is waxen great</u>* [has greatly increased]*before the face of the LORD, and the LORD hath sent us to destroy it.* Gen 19:1-13*

This begs the question: why did God destroy Sodom? We will first deal with what the bible actually reveals to us, and later, we will deal with the false religious teachings that have arisen in a vain effort to legitimize the sin of homosexuality by attempting to discredit the Sodom account.

As we look at the Sodom story, we must explore the facts. The first fact is that no one can deny that gay men lived in Sodom. Although we do not know the population numbers exactly, we can deduce that many of the old and the young males were gay, and a large number of them showed up at Lot's home. This is evident because of the following excerpt from verse 4 in chapter 19 that says:

> *"...the men of the city, even the men of Sodom compassed the house round, both old and young, all the people from every quarter..."*

The phrases seem to imply that all of the men who lived in the city had gathered there. Let's give the benefit of the doubt that this is hyperbole; that does not preclude that we are being told that the number of gay men assembled at Lot's home was plentiful. Although they were unaware that the visitors were angels, they had gathered there because they wanted to have sex with them. It is possible that some showed up simply to watch. But in spite of the fact that there was never an opportunity for any sexual interaction, there is no doubt that there were those in the crowd who had sought homosexual sex.

The next fact, considering the large number of obviously homosexual males who had gathered at Lots house, is that no one else other than Lot and his family were deemed "righteous" by God, an estimation that is recorded in Genesis chapter 18 verses 21-33. A partial excerpt of that passage is shown below as a conversation between God and Abraham before the angels had entered Sodom:

> *And the men rose up from thence, and looked toward Sodom: and Abraham went with them to bring them on the way. And the LORD*

said, Shall I hide from Abraham that thing which I do; Seeing that Abraham shall surely become a great and mighty nation, and all the nations of the earth shall be blessed in him? For I know him, that he will command his children and his household after him, and they shall keep the way of the LORD, to do justice and judgment; that the LORD may bring upon Abraham that which he hath spoken of him. And the LORD said, Because the cry of Sodom and Gomorrah is great, and because their sin is very grievous; I will go down now, and see whether they have done altogether according to the cry of it, which is come unto me; and if not, I will know. And the men turned their faces from thence, and went toward Sodom: but Abraham stood yet before the LORD. And Abraham drew near, and said, Wilt thou also destroy the righteous with the wicked?

The basic idea of this passage when you read the rest of the account is that God promised Abraham that He would not destroy the cities of the plain if He could find just ten righteous people among them. The cities were Sodom, Gomorrah, Admah, Zeboiim, and Bela which was also called Zoar.[74] Although God had originally determined to destroy Zoar too, He spared that city simply because Lot at first intended to evacuate to it and therefore had asked Him for mercy for it since it was a small one. Later on however, Lot changed his mind about staying there in fear. But

Zoar got a reprieve anyway because of the mercy and protection that God had given it for Lot's sake.[75]

Since the minimum of ten righteous people could not be found in the entire plain, the angels hastily escorted Lot and his family out of Sodom. There is no question that the homosexual men along with the rest of the residents were not righteous. Out of the five cities, only four people from Sodom were spared; Lot, his wife, and his two daughters, as were the citizens of Zoar thanks to Lot's intercession. So we conclude that many of the men who lived in the city of Sodom and perhaps even the rest of the cities were homosexual, and that they were not considered righteous by God.

A third fact is that Lot judged their homosexual desires to be very wicked and perverse. He considered their desires so wicked until he offered to exchange his daughters in place of the visitors because he considered that offer a less wicked alternative than the act of men having sex with other men.

The men of Sodom became angry over the idea that a foreigner would come into their city and then judge their behavior. They protested his judgment of their actions and had taken offense to it. Does that not sound like a familiar theme today? The men rejected Lot's alternative offer of the women and threatened to satisfy their desires on him instead in retaliation. In conclusion, Lot judged those men as wicked because of their desire to have sex with his male guests. God had already judged them as unrighteous and did not object to Lot's opinion of them. God also considered them worthy of the judgment of

destruction. Destruction is a decision and a preroga-
tive of God and not of people. So any talk of judgment of this nature exists only because God, being
sovereign, brought it to that level, and not because of
any estimation on the part of readers of the account.
As a matter of fact, we had just read that Abraham
tried to talk God out of destroying them which is
what Godly people will do in prayerful intercession.
The problem was that the minimum number of ten
righteous people that Abraham proffered was not
found. God, being the sovereign Creator, will bring
it to that level on any basis He chooses.

The Commandment against Homosexuality

There is a similar incident recorded in the bible
in the book of Judges but we will first go back to
the book of Leviticus and study the commandments
given to Israel which forbids sexual activity between
men. They are:

*Thou shalt not lie with mankind, as with wom-
ankind: it is abomination.* Leviticus 18:22

*If a man also lie with mankind, as he lieth
with a woman, both of them have committed
an abomination: they shall surely be put
to death; their blood shall be upon them.*
Leviticus 20:13

These are quite plain—except to those who are
bent on doing differently. Let's remember that in the

previous chapter of this book, we learned that God gave the commandments to Moses, who transmitted them first to the elders of Israel who then relayed them to the other leaders down the line until they were received by all the people. So when he says that "you shall not lie with a male as one who lies with a woman," his commandment is first to the elders, then to the thousands of men under them, and so forth. Now the question is—what does this mean? It actually means what it says. The edict is to all men that they should not do with a man what was intended for a man to do with a woman and that is have sex, since "the woman was made for the man." Men are not created to have sex with men, but women are created for men to have sex with, and then God commands that the woman must be a wife, else the sex is still sin. Violation of this created order is disgusting to God. The word abomination means "extremely disgusting," and rightly so, considering the biology of men and women. The phraseology of the verse also implies that since a man is not a female, he shouldn't receive a man sexually with his body in any manner because that is the specific design of females. A male was never intended to be a sexual substitute or option for males. The bible is very clear that God made the woman for the man and that has not changed, nor is there any indication in the bible that God has or would ever change in that respect.

A very important point that can be made here is this: God condemned the act of males having sex with males in those two passages, a point that is reluctantly confirmed by two religious proponents of homosexuality. In the book, <u>What the Bible *Really* Says About Homosexuality</u>, Dr. Daniel Helminiak first implied that Leviticus 18:22 is obscure. But then he writes on the same page,

> "There is no doubt that the text refers to male homogenital acts . . ."

The term "homogenital" means sexual acts between individuals of the same sex, whether male or female. Nevertheless after first claiming that the texts were obscure, he contradicted himself using the words "no doubt" and stating that the verse refers to "homogenital" acts between men.[76]

Of Leviticus 18:22, John Boswell in his book, <u>Christianity, Social Tolerance, and Homosexuality,</u> writes that the ". . .enactments against homosexual behavior characterize it unequivocally as ceremonially unclean rather than inherently evil" in the Greek Septuagint.[77] But along with his vain attempt to diminish the severity of the sin by his contradictory wording, he acknowledged that they are truly prohibitions against homosexual behavior.[78] Unfortunately, Boswell changed the meaning of what he read. God does not merely consider the acts *unclean*, which is very much true while being grossly evil in themselves, although God did not use the word in the texts. "Unclean" is Boswell's word in his explanation. God called homosexual behavior *abominable*, a characterization that demonstrates His greater distaste for the acts than if they were *only* unclean. Another mistake that he made is concluding that the prohibition was just for the Jews.[79] Those sins were the very reasons that the natives of Canaan were being expelled, and by them the land was defiled.[80] Where God was concerned, male/male sex was a capital offense in Israel and violators were, by His orders, to be executed.

Gibeah

Now the incident that took place at Gibeah can teach us more valuable lessons against homosexuality and ungodly sexual encounters. In this incident, we do not see God's summary intervention. Instead, God was sought only through man's desire to avenge an atrocity that took place. One main reason for this is that at this time the Torah had already been given, and although Israel's governing structure was in its developmental stage, God had appointed judges to rule Israel, help them militarily, and to carry out His purposes and judgments.[81]

Earlier, we had learned of the appointments of the elders and heads of families to assist Moses in his leadership of Israel. He was the chief judge when God had appointed him, and the elders and heads of families were also judges under his authority.[82] The responsibility of the judges was to rule the nation and to execute judgment according to God's laws. Sometimes however, we read where judges were not available and people tended to make their own judgments.[83] This kind of existence was a situation where devastating consequences were possible. When God gave Israel His righteous laws of government, He had also given the authority to enforce it. For that reason He raised up judges. As a result, we do not see exactly the same kind of direct intervention from God in the incident at Gibeah as we do with Sodom.

Now the Gibeah story in Judges chapter 19, goes like this: A Levite (a member of the Israelite family of Levi) had a concubine (servant-wife) who was unfaithful to him by having an affair. Afterwards, she returned home to her father. The Levite, wanting her back, searched for her and after finding her at her father's house, was ready to return home but did not because it had gotten too late. He had been delayed by her father who had persuaded him to stay for a few days longer. He finally did leave, but it was late and they (he, his concubine, and another servant) could not continue to travel safely. Rather than stay in Jebus (the name of the city which would later be called Jerusalem) which he thought might be unfriendly to him, he decided to continue on to Gibeah. When they arrived there, they were going to stay outdoors in the square of the city but an old man came along and convinced them to stay with him. After they settled at the old man's home, word had somehow gotten around town that there was a new male visitor in town. Several men who belonged to the Israelite family of Benjamin showed up and demanded that the men bring out the Levite so that they could have sex with him. This desire was a clear violation of the law of God that had been given to the Israelites. Either the Benjamites had failed to teach their children the laws of God which is sin, or the children failed to adhere to those laws when they grew up which is also sin, and sin generates more sin. As Lot did in the Sodom incident, the old man judged their intentions to be wicked—again, not because they wanted to "rape" the man, but because those men wanted sex with another man. We can make that conclusion based on his reply that is found in the following excerpt of the incident.

> *Now as they were making their hearts merry, behold, the men of the city, certain <u>sons of Belial</u>* [worthless men], *beset the house round about, and beat at the door, and spake to the master of the house, the old man, saying, Bring forth the man that came into thine house, that we may <u>know him</u>* [have sex with him]. *And the man, the master of the house, went out unto them, Nay, my brethren, nay, I pray you, do not so wickedly; seeing that this man is come into mine house, do not <u>this folly</u>* [such a foolish, evil thing – a *nebalah*!]. *Behold, here is my daughter a maiden, and his concubine; them I will bring out now, and humble ye them, and do with them what seemeth good unto you: but unto this man do not so vile a thing.* Judges 19:22-24*

Like Lot, the old man was willing to sacrifice his virgin daughter and the man's concubine in order to protect the Levite from what he considered a repulsive act – male on male sex! He judged it more acceptable for them to do what they wanted to do sexually to the women rather than to the men. Both Lot and this old man considered the idea of sex between men more horribly repulsive than the abuse of a woman, and both tried to prevent the homosexual intentions with a suggestion that seemed more appropriate to them. They were more willing to tolerate them forcing sex with the women than forcing sex with a man. Then he judged their desire as evil by calling it "an act of folly "—a *nebalah,* which is the Hebrew word in the feminine sense for foolishness or a foolish act that is 'morally wicked.' I find it interesting that the feminine form of the word is used to describe what those men had desired to do. Another noted fact is that in the very beginning, those men were referred to as "sons of Belial" or worthless men. When a person was given that designation, it meant that they were horribly wicked and lawless. The bible teaches us that a lawless individual lacks the guidance of the law of God and lives as he or she pleases with total disregard for God and His instruction.

Since he saw a dangerous situation developing, and since the men refused to listen to his plea, the old man grabbed the Levite's concubine, pushed her outside, and secured his door. Unlike the Sodom incident, there were no angels for protection and the men settled for the woman and gang raped her all night long, costing the woman's life. She lay dead in the old man's doorway the next morning. Later, the Levite picked up his dead concubine, put her on one of his donkeys, and angrily went home. He had been willing to forgive her of unfaithfulness and bring her back home, but now his long journey had been for nothing.

When he got home, he cut her into twelve pieces and sent each throughout Israel to each of the other tribes of Israel with a note explaining what had happened. The rest of Israel was so enraged until they decided to muster up an army in order to exact justice against the perpetrators of the tribe of Benjamin who had committed this heinous crime. When they arrived in Gibeah, they simply asked the leaders there to turn the perpetrators over to them, but the leaders refused. The leaders had now become accessories to the sinful crime and perhaps they were even part of the crowd that evening. God orchestrated the events to follow so that almost all of the men of Gibeah were destroyed and the city decimated because of the evil deed that was done.

Now here are the synopses that we have so far: first, we have the account of Sodom. We have already established that God considered the entire city wicked because of the discussion He had with Abraham. Unfortunately, only Lot, his wife, and his daughters, qualified to be saved out of the city. A huge problem for proponents of homosexuality is that Lot, who considered the desire of the men who wanted to have sex with the male visitors to be wicked, is characterized as righteous in 2 Peter 2:7. If homosexual sex was a righteous act in God's estimation, then why would Lot be judged a righteous man when he repudiated it? And why would he be judged righteous even though he wanted to sacrifice his daughters in lieu of his male guests?

Secondly, we saw two biblical passages in Leviticus that specifically says that the act of a man engaging in intercourse with another man is abominable before God and punishable by death, which is another huge problem for said proponents. We established that this command was one that came from God directly and was not an invention of Moses. We also learned in the previous chapter that man had sinful desires even before God revealed them as being sinful. Therefore, it is easy to see how God would disdain homosexual acts even before He revealed it to man through His law.

Thirdly, in the Gibeah incident, we have the same kind of reaction from the old man regarding the idea of men having sex with men that we got from Lot. He too offered women instead, knowing that they wanted to have sex with his male visitor, and implied that men having sex with females was far more acceptable than men having sex with his male guest under any circumstances. So from the beginning homosexuality has gotten a negative reaction from righteous people in the bible, as well as from God! In no place in scripture does homosexuality receive positive commentary.

Temple Prostitutes

Now we will discuss scriptural passages that some so-called bible teachers misuse because they attempt to exchange the repudiation of homosexuality with idolatry where the passages in fact denounce homosexuality.

In each of the following scriptural passages, the English word *whore* is translated from the Hebrew root *zanah* which was defined in chapter 4 as meaning *"To go a whoring, commit fornication, be a harlot, serve other gods."* We established that the meaning did not strictly refer to "temple prostitutes" as some would erroneously state, but that the word could simply refer to any kind of sexual fornication, adultery, or idolatry.

This verse is a definite reference to temple prostitution:

Thou shalt not bring the hire of a whore, or the price of a dog, into the house of the LORD thy God for any vow: for even both these are abomination unto the LORD thy God. Deuteronomy 23:18

One thing that God did not want his people to do is commit sexual sin for payment (prostitution), and then bring any portion of that money to the temple for an offering to God. This meant money made by either female or male prostitution. The "price of the whore" had to do with females. The "price of a dog" had to do with males, which makes sense, especially when we look at the following scripture references and the explanation of them:

1) God forbade fathers to prostitute their daughters for money.
   Do not prostitute thy daughter, to cause her to be a whore; lest the landfall to whoredom, and the land become full of wickedness. Lev 19:29

139

2) God forbade priests to marry women who were
   known to be whores, meaning women who were
   sexually promiscuous for any reason.
   They shall not take a wife that is a whore, or
   profane; neither shall they take a woman put
   away from her husband: for he is holy unto
   his God Lev 21:7

The girl a priest married had to be a virgin, no
exceptions. If a girl had sex just once outside of marriage, she was a whore. She could not be a divorcee,
either.

3) If a priest's daughter gave up her virginity before
   she married, she could be executed in a fiery
   death. God demanded a priest's daughter to be an
   example to the rest of the girls in Israel. This and
   the last passage both used the Hebrew word *zanah*
   and had no reference to "temple prostitution" at
   all, but rather to promiscuity and being sexually
   active before marriage. The scripture reference
   under the next item will bear that fact out.
   And the daughter of any priest, if she pro-
   fane herself by playing the whore, she pro-
   faneth her father: she shall be burnt with fire.
   Lev 21:9

4) If it was discovered that a young girl lost her
   virginity before she was married, she could be
   executed.
   Then they shall bring out the damsel to the
   door of her father's house, and the men of

her city shall stone her with stones that she die: because she hath wrought folly in Israel, to play the whore in her father's house: so shalt thou put evil away from among you. Deut 22:21

As we learned before, that means that even if she only had one sexual experience before she was married, she was deemed a whore, and if it was discovered by her new husband that she was not virtuous and it angered him, he could divorce her, and afterward she could be executed for not being virtuous. Again, we see the words, "wrought folly," which means that the act of losing her virginity was also a *nebalah* – a foolish act.

Sex outside of marriage was completely condemned under all circumstances. The fact that it was done for money did not change that position. Based on the law of God, it was sin to engage sexually outside of marriage for any reason. The act of bringing the money to God did not make it any better because of the sinful manner in which it was earned, and when that act was committed it made the money abominable (disgusting) where God was concerned. So if a man had sex with a man, that act was considered abominable. When a man earned money in that abominable manner, and then attempted to bring a portion of those wages to God as an offering, his oblation did not make it any more acceptable. Now that was a common practice associated with idolatry and God did not want it in Israel at all. The <u>Keil & Delitzsch Commentary</u> tells us that prostitution in

Israel was not to be tolerated at all, especially the kind that was related to idol worship. The commentary explained that the "hire of a whore" was the price that a female prostitute (kadeshah) received for her "services" (no pun intended), and the "price of a dog" was the money received by male prostitutes (kadesh) who received wages for their sexual activities related to idol worship. The male prostitutes were given that term because of the vulgar dog-like sexual behavior that their illicit activities resembled.[84]

Any sexual sin is evil, whether done in idolatry, or apart from idolatry. Idolatry is one evil by itself, and sexual sin is another evil by itself. There are many people today who regularly attend church who commit sexual sins. Some engage in sex outside of marriage, or sex in cohabitation (living together) without the benefit of marriage. Such behavior is prevalent among church people who put their sexual feelings and desires ahead of God and His word. According to the word of God that is also a form of idolatry because anything that supplants God is idolatrous. Many individuals who commit such sins do not realize their greater error when they commit sexual sin and then turn around and judge against others who commit other sexual sins.

Thus, the temple prostitute was either a woman who committed sexual sins for money, who would offer proceeds from her acts as offerings to that idol, or a man who committed sexual sins of homosexuality for oblations to give to his idol. God did not want this practice in Israel for any reason because such a practice would completely pollute his people.

New Testament Teaching on Homosexuality

The New Testament has several other references that denounce homosexuality. Here is the first one:

> *Or do you not know that the unrighteous will not inherit the kingdom of God? Do not be deceived; neither fornicators, nor idolaters, nor adulterers, nor effeminate, nor homosexuals* . . . 1 Corinthians 6:9 NASU

From the beginning, this verse sets the tone for all that it has to say by listing some items into the "unrighteous" category. The words on which we will focus our attention are *effeminate* and *homosexual.* Now, as was stated before, the word *homosexual* is a word that was not used in the translation of the King James Bible because at that time the word did not exist. The translators of those days used the phrase "abusers of themselves with mankind" to describe sexual activity between men. The translators of the New American Standard Bible used the modern word *homosexuals* instead of the ancient phrase. The word translated *effeminate* seems somewhat obvious in English, but its real meaning is derived from the language from which both words are translated—Greek.

The first word of the passage, *effeminate,* comes from the Greek word *malakoi* which by one definition means "soft to the touch" or "delicate,"[85] and is used figuratively of a *catamite*. The <u>Webster's Random House Dictionary</u> defines catamite as a "boy or youth who is in a sexual relationship with a man." Greek mythology tells a story of a young boy named Ganymede who was a shepherd boy taking care of a flock when he was spotted by Zeus. Zeus supposedly turned into an eagle, swooped down, and took Ganymede to Mount Olympus where he became a cupbearer to the gods and the boy-lover of Zeus. The myth is considered to be one used by Plato to justify his feelings for some of his male students.[86] Anyway, this myth describes what *malakoi* is, that is, soft and thus effeminate or feminine acting in nature. The catamite was "soft" and took on a feminine character, thus he was described in the Greek language as *malakoi*. The main idea of *malakoi is* that of a male taking on the role of a female, especially the sexually passive role during a sexual encounter.[87]

A closer look at 1 Corinthians 6:9 gives us the picture of what the Holy Spirit is saying to us through the Apostle Paul about the behavior of the unrighteous. He points out that they are unrighteous based on the things they do, and thus delineates them by their acts:

1) Fornicators (because of their sexual activity being unmarried)
2) Idolaters (because of the worship of false gods)
3) Adulterers (because of extramarital activity)
4) Effeminate (because of male homosexual fornication)
5) Homosexuals (also because of male homosexual fornication)
6) Thieves (for stealing)

7) Covetous (for strong passions for, and indulgence in things one cannot lawfully indulge in)
8) Drunkards (for intoxication)
9) Revilers (for using harsh and abusive language)
10) Swindlers (for cheating, scamming, and extorting)

We can conclude then that the *effeminate* (malakoi) are unrighteous, and will not inherit the kingdom of God. But just what does the term mean? Is it limited to just boys who have sex with men? No. The term has more to do with the act of being sexual in a way that only a female should be sexual—that of receiving a penis with his body, however he does so. Only females are anatomically designed by God for that purpose, and no one can scientifically or intelligently argue against that. God didn't create homosexuals, or men to receive a penis from another man in any way. Thus Leviticus 18:22 and Leviticus 20:13 use the following phraseology:

Lev 18:22 Thou shalt not lie with mankind, as with womankind. . .

Lev 20:13 If a man also lie with mankind, as he lieth with a woman...

The implication is that the man receiving the penis sexually in any manner is acting in the stead of a woman, and that is an act that is forbidden by God. Conversely, the man having sex with another man is doing with a man what should only be done with a woman, so the verses make sense either way. A man was not designed to receive a penis in any sexual manner. The word of God is stating plainly that receiving a penis is a female sexual function. When a man is sexual with a man, he is doing what was designed and intended by God for woman to do with a man because she was biologically made for that purpose having been given a specific physical organ to accommodate a man. God does not consider male/male sexual activity as either a substitute, preference, or an option under any circumstance, romantic feelings notwithstanding. I believe that the Holy Spirit inspired such biblical language so that the truth can be made clear to us. The *malakoi is* the man who allows himself to be penetrated sexually by another man in an act of unrighteousness; the person who engages in this behavior and never repents will not inherit God's kingdom. This concept wholly agrees with the Leviticus injunctions. Thus, homosexual desire is self-made, not God-made.

Now what about the word *homosexual*? We understand that the word is a (relatively) new term to describe the behavior of same-sex attraction. In Webster's Random House Dictionary it is defined as "sexual desire or behavior directed towards a person or persons of one's own sex." The New American Standard Updated Bible, translates the Greek word *arsenokoites* as *homosexuals,* which according to Strong's Exhaustive Concordance is a compound word from the Greek words *arsen* and *koites* meaning 'man' and 'bed'.[88] Now the word 'bed' in this case is a sexual term just as it is sometimes a sexual term in

English i.e. "They went to bed with each other" or, "She was caught in bed with him." We clearly understand those phrases to be sexual terminology. The same is no less true for *arsenokoites,* a Greek sexual term that defines and was understood by Greeks to be male/male sexual activity, specifically referring to the active partner who has intercourse of some form with another male as he ordinarily should have in all propriety with a female.[89] He may even utilize some other implement as a substitute during this activity. Regardless, the Holy Spirit condemns all such acts as sinful behavior. Whether a man strictly has same-sex inclinations, or is normally heterosexual but is experimentally engaging in male/male sexual activity, or if he considers himself bi-sexual—if he engages in sex with another man for any reason or under any circumstances, he is unrighteous and guilty of sin and as a result cannot inherit the kingdom of God without repentance.

1 Timothy

This passage confirms the position of the Torah where male/male sex is concerned.

[R]ealizing the fact that law is not made for a righteous person, but for those who are lawless and rebellious, for the ungodly and sinners, for the unholy and profane, for those who kill their fathers or mothers, for murderers and immoral men and homosexuals and kidnappers and liars and perjurers,

and whatever else is contrary to sound teaching. . . I Timothy 1:9-10 NASU*

In Paul's statement he wrote that the Torah is good if it is used properly, and that its primary purpose is that it is written for the unrighteous, which all of us Christians were at one point in our lives before turning to Jesus for forgiveness. Paul used the present tense to teach this position, putting forth the list in the preceding passage to reveal what unrighteousness is from God's point of view. This list will be repeated from the King James Version of the bible. Paul wrote that the Torah was made for:

1) The lawless and disobedient (those who refuse God's standards and defiantly disobey Him)
2) The ungodly and sinners (everybody)
3) The unholy and profane (the aim of the fourth of the Ten Commandments)
4) Murderers of fathers and murderers of mothers (the aim of the fifth commandment)
5) Manslayers (murderers—the aim of the sixth commandment)
6) Whoremongers (men who commit sinful sexual acts—the aim of the seventh commandment)
7) Those who defile themselves with mankind (arsenokoites/homosexuals—the aim of Lev. 18:22; 20:13)
8) Menstealers (kidnappers—the aim of the eight and the tenth commandments)
9) Liars (the aim of the ninth commandment)

10) Perjured persons (lying under oath—the aim of the third commandment)
11) Any *other* thing that is contrary to sound doctrine (the aim of all the commandments)

We can see that this list refers to most of the Ten Commandments, and to commandments in Leviticus. The Apostle Paul declared that all of those are moral laws which have not been abrogated. Two things immediately stand out here. One, is that it again shows us the purpose of the Torah, that it was made for the unrighteous (which includes all of us) to reveal to us what unrighteousness is while we are still in it. The second thing is the fact that along with all that is in the 'blacklist,' homosexuality (designated by the old-world phraseology *"abusers of themselves with mankind"* in the bible), is also blacklisted and it is considered to be contrary to sound doctrine.

Jude

The book of Jude which consists of only one chapter gives us probably the most damning statement and reason for the destruction of Sodom. The seventh verse reads:

Even as Sodom and Gomorrha, and the cities about them in like manner, giving themselves over to fornication, and going after strange flesh, are set forth for an example, suffering the vengeance of eternal fire. Jude 7

The reference is to the angels of Noah's time who, as described in an earlier chapter, sinned by not staying in their proper God-given place but who instead abandoned their boundaries and sought sex and even marriage with humans, and perpetrating violence at the same time. These angels are bound and are currently awaiting judgment. A comparison is drawn to the people of Sodom, who like those angels committed immorality of the worst kind and went "after strange flesh." The idea of going "after strange flesh," and "not staying in their proper God-given place," (Jude 6) are where the parallel is drawn. The men of Sodom did not stay in their proper God-given place but instead went outside of the natural boundaries set by God where sexuality was concerned and were completely given over to a homosexual (strange flesh) lifestyle. The Greek word coined for that depth of immorality is *ekporneuo* which means to be totally given over to fornication. Thayer's Greek Lexicon says that the prefix *ek* "seems to indicate a lust that gluts itself' and "satisfies itself completely."[90] The part of the story fitting this description is where the men wanted sex with the visitors who unbeknownst to them were actually angels. Thus, the men of Sodom in their hearts lusted after other men and defied the natural female boundaries God had otherwise set, preferring males or "strange flesh" in the eyes of God. Therefore Jude says that Sodom and Gomorrah are set forth as an example of the punishment of eternal fire for such sinful behavior symbolized by the method God used to punish the city—fire and brimstone. Further, you will notice that Jude calls their behavior "fornica-tion," which is not rectifiable by marriage because God will not join women with women, or men with men. Neither did He join the women with the angels in the days preceding the flood, although the angels were said to have "married" some of them.

Chapter Seven

ROMANS 1

The Gospel

*N*ow we will discuss Romans chapter 1. This chapter has been severely butchered in defense of homosexual behavior probably because this chapter easily shows the sinfulness of it. We will look at the entire context of the passage in order to properly ascertain its meaning. It reads:

> *For the wrath of God is revealed from heaven against all ungodliness and unrighteousness of men, who hold the truth in unrighteousness; Because that which may be known of God is manifest in them; for God hath shewed it unto them. For the invisible things of him from the creation of the world are clearly seen, being understood by the things that are made, even his eternal power and Godhead,*

so that they are without excuse: Because that, when they knew God, they glorified him not as God, neither were thankful; but became vain in their imaginations, and their foolish heart was darkened Professing themselves to be wise, they became fools, And changed the glory of the uncorruptible God into an image made like to corruptible man, and to birds, and fourfooted beasts, and creeping things. Wherefore God also gave them up to uncleanness through the lusts of their own hearts, to dishonour their own bodies between themselves: Who changed the truth of God into a lie, and worshipped and served the creature more than the Creator, who is blessed for ever. Amen. For this cause God gave them up unto vile affections: for even their women did change the natural use into that which is against nature: And likewise also the men, leaving the natural use of the woman, burned in their lust one toward another; men with men working that which is unseemly, and receiving in themselves that recompence of their error which was meet. And even as they did not like to retain God in their knowledge, God gave them over to a reprobate mind, to do those things which are not convenient; Being filled with all unrighteousness, fornication, wickedness, covetousness, maliciousness; full of envy, murder, debate, deceit, malignity whisperers, Backbiters, haters of God, despiteful, proud, boasters, inventors of evil things, disobedient to parents, Without understanding, covenant breakers, without natural affection, implacable, unmerciful: Who knowing the judgment of God, that they which commit such things are worthy of death, not only do the same, but have pleasure in them that do them. Rom 1:18-2:1

This passage is about the gospel—the good news of salvation and eternal life through Jesus Christ, which is God's main purpose for all of mankind. Paul opens this section in verse 16 by saying that he is not ashamed of the message of the gospel of Christ because it is through that message that we all can be saved and receive eternal life through repentance and forgiveness of sins. But the flip side of salvation is the wrath of God—eternal punishment for sinning against God by ignoring or rejecting his offer of eternal life and deliverance from sin. The reason is that God's standard for living is the highest and best for mankind. It makes sense that He who made the world and the people in it would know what is best for all. As we have seen thus far, failure to live up to His righteous standards is not only called sin, but it also creates unnecessary trouble and hardship for us, a fact that is very difficult to argue with, and no one can deny that the world is filled with problems. A close comparison of the problems that exist and the concepts taught in the scriptures will reveal to anyone willing to acknowledge truth that many of the world's problems are the result of the violations of those concepts. The gospel is designed to deliver us from sin by redemption through the blood of Jesus Christ, and ultimately give us an eternity that will be free from sickness, sorrow, pain, hardship, problems, and death. Now that is really good news! But in order to receive that kind of existence, we must repent from sin and then live by His standards of righteousness that are taught in His word.

Suppression of Truth

Paul also taught in that passage that the wrath of God is revealed from heaven against the ungodliness and unrighteousness of men who suppress truth, which is a scathing indictment against all who reject God. The Holy Spirit through the Apostle Paul is saying to us that we actually know what some basic truths are already—even if we do not want to admit it—because God has revealed those truths to us intrinsically through nature. We can all identify with such truth when we hear it, but some of us reject it anyway. This rejection of truth is actually suppression of truth, which is more than simply not knowing or understanding it because God made us much more discerning than we sometimes pretend to be. Paul, a man formerly known as Saul of Tarsus, who fought against Jesus and the gospel and continued to do so until he had a supernatural encounter with Him while on the way to Damascus to get permission from its officials to arrest any believer-in-Christ he encountered, certainly understood suppression of truth.[91] Paul could admit that he understood what the truth about Jesus was, but being unrighteous and willfully disobedient, he chose to reject any truth about Jesus that was obvious and suppress it with his Pharisaic beliefs. But after his supernatural encounter with Jesus, he could no longer resist that truth. Paul's answer to Jesus when Jesus appeared to him is interesting. Jesus asked, "Paul, why are you persecuting me?" Paul replied, "Who are you Lord?" Jesus answered again, "I am Jesus whom you are persecuting."[92] Paul was indeed astonied, but more so because he *really* knew what the truth was from the beginning. The idea that Jesus was the promised Messiah had already circulated throughout Judea. Jesus had performed numerous miracles and had created quite a stir, and then died on the cross, and then it was rumored that He rose again. Paul simply chose not to believe it, but rather to suppress it, without any investigation at all. The point is that he knew that Jesus had been called the Messiah. He had no doubt heard or perhaps even saw miracles because after all, he was a Pharisee. He could not say that it was never plain enough to be understood because that is the very thing he fought against.

Any idea that God cannot transmit truth clearly is ludicrous. The problem is not God's ability to transmit truth, but rather our unwillingness to receive it. There are truths that God has revealed to people. If they say they don't believe them, it is because they are choosing to suppress them, despite the fact that they are compelling. The passage presented from Romans 1 speaks of knowing the truth, and then suppressing it in favor of unrighteousness.

A very good example of suppression of truth is found in a verbal exchange between Jesus and the Pharisees. Upset over Jesus' shutting down the dishonest profiteering that took place in the temple, the Pharisees sharply questioned Jesus as to who gave Him the authority to do what He did. Jesus responded with a question, promising to answer their question if they answered His. He simply asked whether the baptizing that John the Baptist did was authorized from heaven or by a religious organization. They huddled and conferred about it for a few seconds, concluding that if they answered that John's authority came from heaven, then Jesus would ask them why they didn't believe his (John's) testimony of Jesus being Messiah. On the other hand, the Pharisees realized that if they answered that John's authority was conferred by man, then the common people would be ready to stone them because those people believed that John was a true prophet. The common people had not suppressed the truth about John the Baptist. Evidently the Pharisees were aware of the same truth but they suppressed it by lying to Jesus answering, "We don't know."[93] They responded like that because their agenda was to eliminate Jesus. Their agenda meant more to them than any truth would or could. When people suppress truth, it is because they have an agenda that is more important to them than anything else—including God. In fact, that agenda becomes their god. Paul further wrote,

Because that which may be known of God is manifest in them; for God hath shewed it unto them. Romans 1:19

So here Paul says that there are things that we know about God because he has made those things perfectly clear to us. The word translated *manifest* comes from the Greek word *'phaneros' which means* "shining" or better yet, "evident." These things are much clearer to us than many people want to admit. Let's face it: sometimes it hurts and is even disappointing to admit truth, but that is no reason not to admit it.

For the invisible things of him from the creation of the world are clearly seen, being understood by the things that are made, even his eternal power and Godhead; so that they are without excuse: Romans 1:20

Now, the contention against unrighteous man is stronger. Paul contends that all people have known some very clear things about God ever since creation and that those things are understood based on what He has made which demonstrate His glorious power and intelligent infinite reasoning. This leaves man with no wiggle room for doubt or justification for his erroneous conceptions. Now for the question: what are the clear things that unrighteous man has known about God since creation? One of those things is His power. Again, the existence of creation is a demonstration of a power. Creation proves that a power created it, and that power had to be wise and knowl-edgeable. An unintelligent power could not have cre-ated an intelligently structured universe. Although known by man, that truth can be suppressed within an unrighteous nature. When a man ignores God's power, authority and wisdom, then he fails to wor-ship Him and acknowledge those attributes, He will not obey God either. Such a failure will eventually manifest itself in many wicked actions. Also, if a person does not worship or obey God, he will be self-centered and lack gratitude and thankfulness for anything God has done for him or her. When that happens, then the following can be the result:

> *Because that, when they knew God, they glorified him not as God, neither were thankful; but became vain in their imagina-tions, and their foolish heart was darkened.* Romans 1:21

The Necessity of Thankfulness

Why should a person give thanks? If one is alive, then he or she is alive by the mercy of God. God owes us nothing and we owe Him everything. We all are born sinners and should be rightly cast into eternal judgment. We are given mercy however, only because God loves us and wants us saved, which is why Jesus died on the cross. The fact that God still wants to give us everlasting life when none of us deserves it is a credit to His goodness. In eternity,

God will wipe away all tears. There will be no more pain, suffering, sickness, or sorrow.

> *For, behold, I create new heavens and a new earth: and the former shall not be remembered, nor come into mind. Isaiah 65:17*

> *And God shall wipe away all tears from their eyes; and there shall be no more death, neither sorrow, nor crying, neither shall there be any more pain: for the former things are passed away.* Revelation 21:4

That alone is plenty to look forward to and praise God for. Our hope is in the salvation that will give us a glorious and permanent existence. Salvation is God's purpose through Christ because He knows the hardships that sin puts us through. This salvation was the hope even of the people who lived in "Old Testament" times, although God had not fully revealed to them exactly how He planned to carry it out.[94]

We worship God for who He is. We praise and thank Him for what He has done, and what He is going to do. When you are in good health, you can thank Him. If things are not going too well at present, you can still thank Him knowing that He has your best interest in mind and that He is going to work out your situation. Thankfulness is a very integral part of worship.

The failure to be thankful is the result of ingratitude, bitterness, or anger that resides within.

Unthankfulness is what drives people away from God and into all sorts of things, a theme that Paul sets forth in this passage. One thing that unthankfulness to God can inspire is idolatry. Unthankful people who suppress the truth of God as Supreme creator can end up worshiping all sorts of other deities. In the process, the idealized deities have the characteristics of humans or other created things due to the suppressed truth about a Creator who is not at all like His creation but is superior to it in every way.

One major reason for homosexuality is a lack of thankfulness. The problem with many gay people is that they do not want to live or behave in the biological manner that God made them for, that is, live and behave in the physically God-designed way of their assigned gender. Some argue that they are just attracted to the sex which they themselves are. Others argue that they are in the wrong body. There are males who contend that they "feel like females inside." Some females claim that they "feel more masculine" and that they are attracted to girls and that they hate what they are. They grow up hating their breasts and their menstruation. They hate their vaginas and curse the way they are made. Men who try to act feminine lack thankfulness for their masculinity. They hate their male organs. They desire breasts and menstruation. Some females who prefer to be masculine try to act more masculine and wear masculine clothes and hairstyles. Because of their hatred for their femininity, they never give thanks. They wake up each day bitter and angry against the God who made them. Others, both males and females, resort to surgical alteration and hormone injections in order to gain the physical appearance of the other sex which they desperately long to become, even though they never actually become a member of the opposite sex, a fact corroborated by medical science. Deceived into thinking that they are living a lie, they end up actually living a lie, denying who and what they are as God made them from a physical perspective, and turning to a lifestyle and sexual behaviors that God did not intend for them, erroneously saying that being gay is what God made them to be. A man who is homosexual is still a man, and a woman who is a lesbian is still a woman. Regardless of what they may think they feel inside, the bible teaches us that God made the woman for the man.

Those longings or desires, which are called *lusts* in the bible, demonstrate attitudes of the lack of thankfulness for what they are, and were really created to be and are the "vain imaginations" spoken of by the apostle Paul. Unthankfulness, says the Holy Spirit through the apostle Paul, is the reason for the "vain imaginations." Those "vain imaginations" (called "futile speculations" in the NASU) are erroneous conclusions that come from a darkened heart; a heart that is darkened by their failure to honor God and be thankful for who and what God really made them to be. There are also women who are not necessarily trying to be or act masculine, and men who are not necessarily trying to be or act feminine. They simply prefer to mate with those of the same sex. Regardless, it's wrong because God made the woman for the man as established earlier and repeated several times. He did not create a *third* sex, or another option for either males or females where sexual mating relationships are concerned.

The Reprobate Mind

Now when people go astray in any area of life, God works hard to keep them from continuing to go in that direction. When people persist, He reluctantly lets them go after their pursuits, even to their destruction, but not without a fight. He struggles against them because He loves them and does not want them to be destroyed. Eventually, the time comes when God gives up the fight with some people. This is what is meant by:

*And even as they did not like to retain God in their knowledge, God **gave them over** to a reprobate mind, to do those things which are not convenient;* Romans 1:28

As people went deeper into idolatry, they would begin to do reprobate things such as sacrifice their children, cut themselves, fornicate, have sexual orgies, or have sex and donate the proceeds to idols. The word *reprobate* is the Greek word *adokimon* which means to be 'unapproved' and 'rejected.' This lack of approval and rejection is by God.

The human mind becomes reprobate because of the thought processes that originate from within that are the result of desires of the body that are unapproved and rejected by the Creator. If a person dies in this condition, then that person is ultimately rejected by the Creator. The Romans 1 passage teaches about practices that people might engage in that were expressly forbidden in Israel by God through the moral commandments of the Torah. The reason that God dispossessed the Canaanites is because they did those things and God purposed to cleanse the land of those behaviors and put His Name there and make it holy. Earlier we showed that homosexual behavior was prohibited in two passages in Leviticus: 18:22 and 20:13. The fuller context of Leviticus 18 is more telling in the following verses:

> *Do not defile yourselves by any of these things; for by all these the nations which I am casting out before you have become defiled. 'For the land has become defiled, therefore I have brought its punishment upon it, so the land has spewed out its inhabitants. 'But as for you, you are to keep My statutes and My judgments and shall not do any of these abominations, neither the native, nor the alien who sojourns among you (for the men of the land who have been before you have done all these abominations, and the land has become defiled);* Leviticus 18:24-27 NASU

So Leviticus 18 shows us that after God warned Israel in detail about what sexual sins they should not commit, He then told them that the people in the land that they were to possess were committing all those sins and that was the reason that God was dispossessing them and replacing them with the Israelites. God expected Israel's behavior to be holy.

Romans 1 is not Exclusively about Idolatry

The mistake made by homosexuals, religious proponents of homosexuality, and religious false teachers is that this passage is only about temple prostitution and idolatry. They contend that homosexual "love" is different from the things mentioned here, and that homosexual love is approved by God because it is "love." A closer look at what Paul has written here says quite differently. Remember, there are certain things that are true that are already known intrinsically by man, based on the way man is made. The aspect of God's nature and intent where natural sexual activity is concerned is already known and understood by people because God has already revealed it to us on the basis of the way we are physically made.

Wherefore God also gave them up to uncleanness through the lusts of their own hearts, to dishonour their own bodies between themselves: Rom 1:24

This passage shows us that they *dishonored* their bodies. How did they dishonor their bodies? They dishonored their bodies through same-sex sexual acts, which Paul states in this passage are also unclean. Idolatry does not dishonor a person's body, but it dishonors God and it is a separate sin in and of itself. Idolatry was committed in conjunction with the sin of their dishonoring their bodies through illicit sexual acts. Same-sex sex will dishonor the human body whether it is accompanied by idolatry or not. Another point that can be made here is that homosexuals contend that God made them to be homosexual, or that they are born that way. But Paul taught that they behave that way because of the desires that originate within their own hearts. God has nothing at all to do with homosexual behavior.

The Road to Homosexuality

Lack of thankfulness to God as the Sovereign can lead to idolatry, which is a spiritual darkness that helps to spawn ritual same-sex sexual immorality since there are no moral standards in idol worship. But outside of idolatry, unthankfulness for the gender and sexual role that God has given to each of us based on our physiology leads to a person's denial of who he or she really is, and defiance against what God really wants. Defiance leads to suppression of truth about their sexual roles and ultimately rebellion against God through lying and justification about how they think they are created and about what God intended them to be. Then finally, the suppression of this truth—the fact that God made the woman for the man which is evidenced by the obvious anatomical genital functions of both the man and the woman— leads to same-sex sexual immorality.

In the case of homosexuals, living for homosexuality and for its agenda are more important than anything else as they are totally consumed by that lifestyle. Hence, they worship and serve others who live for, accept, and promote that agenda who are far more important to them than anything God may want them to know or understand. Hence, the homosexual lifestyle is in itself idolatry.

The Truth of God

Who changed the truth of God into a lie, and worshipped and served the creature more than the Creator, who is blessed for ever. Amen. Rom 1:25

The truth of God is that when God makes a man a man, He expects him to function in the way that He intended for a man to function. When He makes a woman a woman, He expects her to function in the way that He intended for a woman to function. Again, God made the woman for the man. When someone denies that, then they are calling that truth a lie. Yet, we know that fact intrinsically by nature. The following is not intended to be vulgar in any way, but informational. The most defining physical aspect of a man are his penis and scrotum. This is how he is defined physically as a man. Those two physical attributes are designed to carry out the intention of God where he said to "be fruitful and multiply and replenish the earth."[95] But the man cannot do that by himself. The woman was made for him to assist God in that purpose. Her most defining physical attributes are her breasts, her vagina, her ovaries, and her womb. Her vagina is a perfectly made receptacle for receiving the sperm produced by the testicles within the male scrotum in order to carry out the blessing of God in reproduction. Again, we know that intrinsically. To deny that and declare that fact untrue is to lie against God's intent and the science of biology. Thus, the truth of God becomes a lie to the dark heart of man while man seeks to justify his own concepts and desires.

> *Professing themselves to be wise, they became fools, And changed the glory of the uncorruptible God into an image made like to corruptible man, and to birds, and fourfooted beasts, and creeping things.* Rom 1:22-23

One of the results of a dark heart is a foolish idea that brings God down to the level of men and creation where He is worshipped in the likeness of an animal, an insect, or a human, rather than as God Almighty who is far above all of His creation. In the same vein, He is even sometimes thought of as having desires or ideas similar to humans. The dark heart says that "God made me gay" thus making God out as though He had a gay mind himself. The other result of a dark heart is that futile conclusions are reached through reasoning away God's truth with man's science under the guise of education and knowledge. The conclusions seem to be arrived at through thorough scientific research, experimentation, and evaluation, or even through "spiritual enlightenment." But those processes are nothing more than intelligent rejection of the truth of God that we already know and understand intrinsically about males and females. Thus man promotes himself as learned and wise, but before God, he has really become a fool.

When people persist in denying truth, and lying about God's intention where His will has been revealed, God does His best to hinder and redirect them. In Genesis, it says that He strives with man. This means that He works very hard attempting to keep man from going against His will.[96]

Gays don't realize it, but the current struggle against the gay lifestyle is coming from God himself, making it difficult for them to promote the lifestyle. God is the one putting up the huge fight to hinder their successes, because He is not willing that any of them should perish because of His love for them. Jesus came to save, not condemn. But condemnation comes to people who prefer to live contrary to the will of God.[97] After a while, God eventually gives up the fight.

Wherefore God also gave them up to unclean-ness through the lusts of their own hearts, to dishonour their own bodies between them-selves: Rom 1:24

The Truth about "The Closet"

The real reason that homosexuals have such a hard time 'coming out of the closet' is not because of the pressures from society, but because of the pres-sure exerted from God who attempts to keep them from resigning to a lifestyle of sin that is contrary to His will. God makes the decision to be homosexual difficult, and urges them through righteous and some public pressure not to continue in that lifestyle. However, God will not force them to reconsider. If they persist, He will let them have their way and give them up to dishonor their bodies. This dishonoring of their bodies is the result of the desires that were already in their hearts—the things that they already wanted to do, despite their God-given understanding of how they are made and what they should do. Little girls know that when they mature, it is normally expected of them to marry and then produce a family. Little boys know that when they mature, it is normally expected of them to find a wife (or wives in some cultures and in the Old Testament) and procreate with them. Society did not create that expectation because it came from God Himself. But within people's hearts a desire can develop for something else other than what God created them for. Deep within their hearts they know that their actions are wrong because of their biology and through pressure from God. Initially, they will keep those desires 'in the closet.' But they will eventually suppress truth in order to follow their intense desires.

Vile Affections

> *For this cause God gave them up unto vile affections: for even their women did change the natural use into that which is against nature:* Romans 1:26

The phrase "vile affections" is more proof that this is not exclusively about idolatry. Paul is referring to their behavior and actions and not idol worship. While idol worship certainly can lead to a lifestyle of vile affections, idol worship is not the only reason that the lifestyle emerges. The phrase that confirms this is: *"for even their women did change the natural use into that which is against nature. . ."* Paul defines "natural use" where sexuality is concerned. Since the scriptures are inspired by the Holy Spirit,[98] there is no doubt that this truth about our sexuality is from God, and there is no doubt that we already know and understand it.

Natural Use

One erroneous idea of that verse says that what Paul meant was that those leaving the "natural use" are those who are born heterosexual but who switch over to the homosexual lifestyle leaving their own "natural use." The contention is that it is "natural" for those persons to be heterosexual so if they do homosexual things, they have sinned. John Boswell wrote:

> ". . . the persons Paul condemned are manifestly not homosexual: what he derogates are homosexual acts committed by apparently heterosexual persons."[99]

Likewise in this convoluted thinking, the person who is homosexual must remain homosexual. If he or she leaves the homosexual lifestyle for the hetero-sexual lifestyle, then they have left their "natures" and have sinned. Such an idea however, is prepos-terous. A close evaluation of the phrase translated from the original Greek language will prove how wrong that idea is.

In Romans 1:26, the phrase "natural use" in the Greek language is a sexual phrase that specifically pertains to women, describing how they had left the God intended "natural use" for that which *is against* or *contrary to nature*. That fact is confirmed by the wording of the text in the original Greek language. The Greek phrase transliterated for the English phrase ". . .change the natural use into that which is against nature" is *meteéillaxan teén fusikeén chreésin eis teén para fúsin.*[100] *Meteéillaxan* literally means "to exchange" or "swap." In that one is trading some-thing for something else. *Fusikeén chreésin* is defined as the "physical sexual use" which specifically refers to the sexual behavior of *women. Para fúsin* means "against" the "genus" or "sort". The genus refers to the class of women, including all women. What Paul was saying is that the women referred to in the verse exchanged or swapped the intended natural sexual physical use of their bodies for another kind of use that is over and above or contrary to that which was expected (from the Creator's point of view) of all women. In other words, when a woman has sex with another woman, that behavior is an exchanged behavior and is contrary to both women. The God intended original use for a woman is a man because the woman was made for the man, and the contrary or exchanged use of a woman is that of being sexual with another woman and that behavior comes from the heart and is unclean before God. To deny that is to suppress truth, and imply that the genuine truth which is of God, is a lie.

To further define "natural use," the 27th verse reemphasizes the original point using the male.

And likewise also the men, leaving [forsaking] *the natural use of the woman, burned in their lust one toward another; men with men working that which is unseemly, and receiving in themselves that recompence* [punishment] *of their error which was meet* [appropriate]. Rom 1:27

The first sentence of Romans 1:27 placed the same phrase of the last verse—"natural use"—of the woman into the context where such acts belong—that is, with a man. In both verses, the idea of "natural use" is from the woman's point of view only. Paul begins in verse 26 decrying the incorrect [sexual] use of the woman which is with another woman, and then ends in verse 27 decrying the men who forsake that same "natural use" to have sex with other men. The comparison is drawn by decrying the women's errors first, then ending with the men's, proving to us that the idea of a "natural" homosexuality is neither expressed nor implied in scripture. This abandoning of women by men, says Paul writing under the inspiration of God's Holy Spirit, is inappropriate and unthinkable, which is the meaning of *unseemly*.

The verses teach us that both women, who exchange the 'natural use' for sex with other women which is against nature, and men, who abandon the same 'natural use' of the woman turning to men for sex instead, live in opposition to God's expectation for them by committing acts that are inappropriate, vile, and dishonoring to the bodies that God gave to them. Paul teaches that those who are engaged in the gay lifestyle have given up the sexuality for which they were physically designed, for another kind of sexuality for which they were not physically designed. He goes on to say that truthfully, all people know these things, because God has revealed them to us through creation. But in order to justify contrary behavior, people will suppress this knowledge in unrighteousness.

Uncleanness

The Romans passage in verse 24 also teaches us that homosexual sex is unclean as well. Homosexual acts are always spiritually unclean and nothing can cleanse them. All who commit such acts, whether they consider themselves to be gay or not, are made unclean by them. Any person who is made unclean by those acts remains unclean before God unless they repent and receive atonement through the blood of Jesus Christ. A marriage ceremony cannot cleanse them because sexual acts between persons of the same sex are always unclean and condemned. Since God never intended for males to have sex with males or females to have sex with females, God does not join them in marriage. Jesus said,

> *. . . Have ye not read, that he which made them at the beginning made them <u>male</u> and <u>female</u>, and said, For this cause shall a man leave father and mother, and shall cleave to his wife: and they twain shall be one flesh? Wherefore they are no more twain, but one flesh. What therefore God hath joined together, let not man put asunder.* Matthew 19:4-6*

Marriage is a relationship validated by God, and not man or civil ceremonies. There is no recourse for a homosexual relationship to be cleansed because God intended for sex to be between a man and a woman who are married to each other. All other kinds of sexual behavior outside of that boundary are always sinful.

Sexual Orientation

Jesus is clear that God made males and females. Paul averred that God made the woman for the man. There are no variances here. Even in cases where individuals are born with ambiguous genitalia, or where there is a chromosomal problem with DNA that may produce genetic problems within different people, while those differences may create some kind of deformity or produce physical problems in individuals, it is always clear that a definite male or female was intended, the deformity notwithstanding. Science has taught us that the basic chromosomal makeup is either XX for females or XY for males. And where the definite sex of the individual was intended, the woman's sexual orientation was designed to be towards a male for she was created for him, and the male's sexual orientation was designed to be towards a female by our Heavenly Creator. To deny this is to suppress His truth and call His truth a lie.

Chapter Eight

OTHER DOCTRINAL REFUTATIONS

*M*any church organizations and religions leaders today have no real concept of the will of God where sexuality is concerned, so they are giving in to the falsehood that homosexuality is somehow acceptable by God because of a misconstrued understanding of the "love" of God.[101] God is indeed love, but not on the bases presented by the many false teachers and theologians who are presenting these erroneous teachings on homosexuality. The presence of a Ph.D does not gurantee that its possessor understands God. The proper understanding of God's love will be dealt with in the final chapter.

Misunderstanding of Sin

Many religious teachers have a false conception of sin and what it is. The proper biblical concept of what sin is was discussed in chapter 2. Religious proponents of homosexuality definitely do not know what sin is for if they did, they would not be attempting to justify what God has called abominable. What lies at the root of the misunderstanding is that most people mistakenly think that sin has to result in something awful. Helminiak, for example, thinks that the scriptures should be expected to show, as he puts it, that "homogenitality or homosexuality" is ". . .harmful, unkind, destructive, unloving, dishonest, unjust. . ." in order to be considered sinful, or that homosexual sex must include any of those elements to be considered wrong. Additionally, in his estimation, if those acts are not "abusive, hurtful, wanton, or lewd," then there is nothing wrong with such behavior.[102]

But as explained in chapter 2 of this book, the very first sin did not fall into any of those categories. Sin is disobeying a directive of God, regardless of what you or I or anyone else think of the result. By the same token, Helminiak also says that there is "no evidence . . . that homosexuality is in any way pathological."[103] I will agree with him that homosexuality is not pathological at all, but neither was Adam and Eve's act of eating the forbidden fruit. Sin is evil because it is a disregard for what God has commanded, and not because it produces an immediate bad or tragic result.

Considering that we are living in the last days (also called the days of the son of man[104]), this chapter should provide a wake-up call to believers as well as those who simply do not know and are caught between the arguments, unaware that dangerous false doctrines and teachings would indeed be prevalent in the days preceding the coming of Christ.[105] And it should also challenge them to rethink their positions. Jesus said that the truth will make you free.[106] Therefore the purpose of this chapter will be to refute the more prominent biblical falsehoods concerning homosexuality and the obvious reasons for the refutations will be presented.

Jesus and Sex

Helminiak, in discussing the text in Matthew 15:10, 18-20 wrote that

". . . Jesus rejected the importance of the Jewish purity laws. The only purity that mattered for Jesus was "purity of heart."[107]

If you are unknowledgeable, such a statement will deceive you. Now the scripture texts that he discussed read like this from the KJV:

Matthew 15:10 And he called the multitude, and said unto them, Hear, and understand: Matthew 15:18-20 But those things which proceed out of the mouth come forth from the heart; and they defile the man. For out of the heart proceed evil thoughts, murders, adulteries, fornications, thefts, false witness, blasphemies: These are the things which defile a man: but to eat with unwashen hands defileth not a man.

179

As was explained in chapter 2, Jesus indeed rejected the man-made traditions that were handed down and given equal status with the Torah by the religious leaders of the day. Those traditions were written in the Talmud. In rejecting them, Jesus said,

> *For laying aside the commandment of God, ye hold the tradition of men, as the washing of pots and cups: and many other such like things ye do.*
> *And he said unto them, Full well ye reject the commandment of God, that ye may keep your own tradition.* Mark 7:8-9

But Jesus never rejected the Torah. Of the Torah He said,

> *For verily I say unto you, Till heaven and earth pass, one jot or one tittle shall in no wise pass from the law, till all be fulfilled.* Matthew 5:18

If God is going to use the Torah as the standard of judgment against the unbelieving world, then Jesus' words makes plenty of sense.

But how does this relate to the "pure in heart"? Jesus listed in Matthew 15:18-20 the things that defile, that is, makes anyone unclean before God. Fornication is one of them. Homosexuals commit the sin of fornication through their sexual acts since fornication is the sin of sex outside of marriage. Jesus taught us plainly in Matthew 19:4-6:

> *And he answered and said unto them, Have*
> *ye not read, that he which made them at the*
> *beginning made them male and female, And*
> *said, For this cause shall a man leave father*
> *and mother, and shall cleave to his wife: and*
> *they twain shall be one flesh? Wherefore they*
> *are no more twain, but one flesh. What there-*
> *fore God hath joined together, let not man put*
> *asunder.*

In that passage, Jesus taught us that God joins men and women. No other marital combination such as male/male, or female/female is ever alluded to, implied, or suggested. No examples of such exist anywhere in scripture, and anytime such combinations are mentioned, they are mentioned only in condemnation. Therefore, God does not join men with men, or women with women in marriage, and He is the final judge of who is and who is not properly married. If indeed God does not join men with men or women with women in marriage, then their subsequent sexual acts are always fornication and in violation of His will, and they are unclean. This is particularly so because the bible is specific that the woman was made for the man.

Those who argue that Jesus never said a word about homosexuality argue so because they are suppressing truth and are refusing to see what Jesus taught concerning marriage. Remember: Paul taught that suppressed truth is the engine that drives homosexuality.

Helminiak's contention that "Jesus was not preoccupied with sex"[108] is also misleading. In His teaching on marriage and divorce in Matthew 19, Jesus is plainly speaking of sex. Now Jesus did not approach sex like this present society does, but He did teach men the truth and the danger about their sinful desires. He also taught that if a man divorces his wife for any reason other than sexual infidelity, the subsequent marital relationship will be adulterous because there would be sex in that relationship too. When people behave contrariwise to what God wants, they have committed sin. Hebrews 13:4 says that God will judge adulterers and he is not kidding. Repentance (turning away from it forever) is the only way out of God's judgment when we are guilty, and sometimes, the repercussions of our sins are still experienced anyway, such as in the case of King David.

Sodom and Gomorrah

Proponents of homosexuality say that the lack of "hospitality" was the reason that God destroyed Sodom and the other plain cities. Helminiak says that ". . . a cardinal rule of Lot's society was to offer hospitality to travelers." He does not in any manner substantiate that 'cardinal' rule. He further states that Sodom's sin was "abuse and offense against strangers," "insult to the traveler," and "inhospitality to the needy." He adds that "When male-male rape becomes part of the story, the additional offense is sexual abuse—gross insult and humiliation in Lot's time and in our own." He opines that the point of this story (inhospitality, etc.) is "understood in its own historical critical context," and that "the author was not concerned about sex in itself."[109]

John Boswell points to attempted rape as a more obvious possibility that has been ignored by biblical scholars of all time. He also writes that inhospitality being Sodom's sin rather than homosexuality has gained increasing favor among scholars since 1955, who, according to him, claim that "the sexual overtones . . . are minor" if they are present at all.[110] The 1955 date refers to the publication year of the book <u>Homosexuality and the Western Christian Tradition</u> by Derrick S. Bailey, who being gay, was the first to twist the scriptures in an effort to re-interpret standard biblical views on the sin of homosexuality. He is the one who introduced the "inhospitality" interpretation of the destruction of Sodom.

Boswell went on to insist that Jesus himself believed that Sodom was destroyed because of inhospitality by quoting Jesus in Matthew 10:14-15 where He says:

> *"And whosoever shall not receive you, nor hear your words, when ye depart out of that house or city, shake off the dust of your feet. Verily I say unto you, It shall be more tolerable for the land of Sodom and Gomorrah in the day of judgment, than for that city.*

Additionally, he promotes that position on his misunderstanding of Jesus' instructions to His disciples that if the people in the cities of the house of Israel do not accept them or their message, i.e are inhospitable to them, then they must "shake off the dust" from their feet against the city, because their judgment will be worse that the judgment that went against Sodom and Gomorrah. In his contention, the belief is that the city was destroyed because of its inhospitality and not for sexual immorality.[111] But the point of Jesus' instruction is about what will be the consequences of the people in the cities who reject the disciples'message of the gospel of the Messiah rather than inhospitality towards them.

The argument used for the "inhospitality" interpretation is derived from a passage in Ezekiel 16:48-49 where it states:

> *As I live, saith the Lord GOD, Sodom thy sister hath not done, she nor her daughters, as thou hast done, thou and thy daughters. Behold, this was the iniquity of thy sister Sodom, pride, fullness of bread, and abundance of idleness was in her and in her daughters, neither did she strengthen the hand of the poor and needy.*

Now verse 50 adds:

> *And they were haughty, and committed abomination before me: therefore I took them away as I saw good.*

Helminiak, with reference to verse 50 says that there are those who see homosexuality in the text in the word *abomination,* because of the comparison that can be drawn between it and Leviticus 18:22. He contends that since *abomination* can refer to many things, the abominable things that it refers to are in verse 49.[112]

Any attempt to minimize or even ignore the sexual aspect of the Sodom story does no justice to the text at all. As was stated in this book in chapter 6, it is evident that Lot took offense to the idea that the man wanted to engage sexually with men and offered, he thought, what was a more appropriate alternative—his daughters. Another problem with the "hospitality" reasoning is even more evident: why would God want to destroy all of the plain cities over the acts of the men in one city? Had they too committed the same "hospitality breach" as the men of Sodom?

Now keep in mind that the account says that "all the men of Sodom" had come to Lot's house demanding that he bring the visitors out that they may "know" them. Helminiak contradicts himself on the subject. First he says that "there is a clear sexual reference in the story,"[113] then he turns around and says "there is no way of being absolutely certain whether this text refers to homogenital acts or not."[114] The reference is clear that the men wanted to do sexual acts with the visitors, and Lot offered them his daughters instead.

Boswell also opines in an unsubstantiated statement that the basis of the inhospitality interpretation is that Lot, being a foreigner, had violated a custom of Sodom by entertaining a foreigner "without obtaining the permission of the elders of the city." Thus, the men of Sodom wanted to 'know' who these men were.[115] Such an explanation is a very weak if not unscholarly attempt to misconsture the verb 'know' to direct the unlearned reader away from the otherwise obvious sexual sense in order to justify an erroneous attempt at validating homosexuality.

The evidence that the verb *know* is sexual in this passage is overwhelming. First of all, the act of wanting to identify men is not in itself a wicked act. Secondly, Lot's response is not consistent with such a request. Lot made a judgment that what they wanted to do was wicked, and his response was that he would rather that they 'know'—that is, have sex— with his daughters instead. The contention that Lot would want them to "identify" his daughters instead of "identifying" the men makes no sense whatsoever. 'Knowing' the men by inquiry would not be a threatening act. Yet, the men threatened to do worse to Lot because he would not cooperate with their original request. Worse than what? And why did they use the word "worse?" If all the men of Sodom wanted to do was find out who these visitors were, that would not have been a problem, and it would have hardly been a reason for God to want to destroy the plain cities. The desires of the men were sexual, Lot's response was disgust, which is a normal response to such a sexual request, and Lot's solution was clearly sexual as well as judgmental. God's response of devastating judgment was also the result of his disgust for what was a disgusting climate that had been festering within the entire plain for some time. Thirdly, the verb *know,* or a form of it is used 18 times in the King James Version of the bible in a sexual context.[116]

'Abhorrent disgust' is the meaning of *abomination,* which is translated from the same Hebrew word used to describe God's attitude toward homosexual acts in Leviticus 18:22 and 20:13. Remember, as was discussed in chapter 6, any act involving sex between males is disgusting to God, no matter what the reason. Both Helminiak and Boswell use Ezekiel 16:48-49 to delineate the sins mentioned as Sodom's problems and contend that there was no improper sexuality involved in the reason for its destruction. The problem with their conclusions is that they refuse to recognize what verse 50 reveals about "abomination."

And they were haughty, and committed abomination before me: therefore I took them away as I saw good.

Without a doubt the abomination, that is, something disgusting, happened *in addition* to the pride, arrogance, and careless ease, and the lack of care for the poor and needy, evidenced by the conjunction *'and'* in verse 50. Since God reveals to us in Leviticus that male/male sex is disgusting (an abomination) to Him, it should be obvious that what the men of Sodom proposed was that disgusting desire — regardless of whether it would transpire in rape or not, and is part of what is meant by *". . .they . . . committed abomination before me . . . "*

One very important fact: Ezekiel revealed a list of why Sodom was destroyed, but does not mention immorality as one of them. But, as pointed out in chapter 6 in this book, Jude 7 plainly and specifically adds immorality to the list of reasons Sodom and the other cities were destroyed:

> *Even as Sodom and Gomorrah, and the cities about them in like manner, giving themselves over to* **fornication**, *and going after strange flesh, are set forth for an example, suffering the vengeance of eternal fire.*

The reason pointed out by Jude is sexual. Jude says that they were totally given over to fornication, which is a defining characteristic of homosexuality because homosexuality cannot ever be anything but fornication. Jude is very clear as to the reason for the destruction of Sodom and the other cities.

David and Jonathan

Religious proponents of homosexuality who erroneously use the bible to justify the gay lifestyle will often point to a passage that feature young David before his reign as king in Israel and his friendship with King Saul's son, Jonathan. David and Jonathan were simply very good friends. Jonathan was ordinarily in line to inherit the throne of his father Saul, but he had long conceded the throne to David because of his faith in God. Jonathan had no animosity whatsoever against David, knowing that David had already been ordained by God to succeed his (Jonathan's) father in his place on the throne. Jonathan was all for David's ascension and harbored no jealousy for the seat of power at all. 1 Samuel 18 shows that Jonathan ceremoniously conceded the throne to David by giving David his robe, weapons, and belt.[117] Homosexuals tend to want to make a sexual gesture out of the passage that shows that concession by erroneously concluding that David and Jonathan had engaged in a sexual act at this time. Such an act is not alluded to, stated, nor implied in that passage. The sexual verb *know* is not mentioned there. The passage says absolutely nothing else except that Jonathan gave David his royal attire and weapons.

Verse 1 of the same chapter says that Jonathan loved David as his own soul. This was pure friendship only and any conclusion that their relationship was sexual is simply unsubstantiated presumption with no evidence or basis in fact. What gay men do not understand is the depth of friendship that two men can have with absolutely no romantic or sexual overtures. Since they tend to have romantic and sexual overtures towards other men, they have difficulty understanding how one man can relate to another in friendship without any sexual desires attached.

Another passage involving David and Jonathan that is misrepresented by religious homosexual proponents is found at 1 Samuel 20:41 which reads:

*And as soon as the lad was gone, David arose
out of a place toward the south, and fell on
his face to the ground, and bowed himself
three times: and they kissed one another, and
wept one with another, until David exceeded.*

Sadly, the proponents of abominable relationships
tend to want to see something here that never existed
at all. They even go so far as to say that the verse as
quoted means that David experienced an orgasm with
Jonathan because of the word "exceeded" in the text.
The greatest problem with this horrible misconcep-
tion is how God could say in His law to Israel to put
men who have sexual intercourse with one another to
death, and then turn around and make a man king of
His people after that man had committed such an act.
God would not have anointed David king of Israel if
he had been homosexual. After David became king,
God did show mercy to him when he should have
been executed in the matter of Bathsheba, but keep in
mind that David's sin is clearly presented, as well as
God's mercy. The purpose of the story of David's sin
is for us is to see God as a God of mercy, who does
not want to destroy, but to save. He simply wants
repentance and a change of heart and lifestyle.

The phrase ". . .until David exceeded" describes
an intense mixed emotional moment for David
wherein he realized that he and his good and loyal
friend must part ways because David had to leave
in order to preserve his life. It was mixed because
of David's realization of Jonathan's loyalty to him
in spite of the fact that David was taking what was

Jonathan's future place, and that Jonathan's loyalty and frienship towards David was unaffected. That realization humbled David and brought him to his knees in a bucket of tears and they wept together. David was emotionally overcome to a greater extent than Jonathan by the gravity of the situation as well as the kindness from Jonathan, hence the verb *exceeded*. One has to understand how serious the situation was at that time. Under normal circumstances, Jonathan should have killed David, and David knew that. But Jonathan loved him as a friend instead. King Saul knew that too and was incensed. His anger was the exact opposite of David's emotions to the extent that he almost killed Jonathan![118] At that point, Saul determined to kill David himself in order to, in his mind, preserve his son's dignity.

Still another passage butchered by religious proponents of homosexuality is the one that occurs after the account where both King Saul and Jonathan were slain in a battle against the Philistines.[119] David sorrowfully laments his friend's death and exclaims woefully, "I am distressed for you, my brother Jonathan; you have been very pleasant to me. Your love to me was more wonderful than the love of women."[120]

The verse only indicates the depth of their friendship and in no way indicates that David and Jonathan had an abominable relationship. Had that been the case, God would have judged them as abominable, David would never have been anointed king, and if discovered, they both would have both been put to death. Furthermore, since David was a significant individual, the bible account would have been clear that such a sin had transpired and would not have hidden it. Moreover, it is a fact that David was Jonathan's brother-in-law by his marriage to Jonathan's sister, Michal. Initially he was very eager to wed Jonathan's sister Merab, knowing that as a result, he would become the king's son-in-law.[121] After Saul broke his original promise to give his oldest daughter Merab to David as a reward for killing the giant, David was willing to risk his life and kill 200 soldiers from the enemy Philistine army to present twice the dowry the king required to marry Michal.[122] As we also learned in chapter 3, David had already amassed *seven* wives for himself when he lusted for Bathsheba who later became his *eighth* wife. David's behavior towards women is hardly the behavior of a man who by the assesment of false religious teachers is supposedly inclined towards homosexuality. A man struggling with homosexuality can barely handle marrying one woman.

In eastern cultures, men have always customarily greeted other men with simultaneous kisses on the cheek, and it is still a major custom for those cultures today. In some circles in America, that custom is also practiced. A former member of the Church of God in Christ, I've greeted many men with kisses on the cheeks. There are ministers who also do the same in other denominations. None of these are homosexual actions, nor do they imply any "latent" tendency towards homosexuality. The bible plainly teaches:

> *Greet all the brethren with an holy kiss.*
> *1 Thessalonians 5:26*

Now I have been kissed on numerous occasions by men, and have kissed numerous men myself. If I simply made the exact same statement without the previous explanation, homosexuals would be eager to read romantic inclinations into my statement, not realizing that such a gesture of greeting, men kissing one another on the cheeks, has no romantic implications at all. That is the nature of what occurred between David and Jonathan, being men of eastern culture and customs.

Ruth and Naomi

Religious proponents who attempt to put a Godly stamp on a lifestyle that God considers abominable have to take scriptures out of context, interpolate, and butcher them in their vain attempt to legitimize homosexuality. In 2 Peter 3:15, Peter wrote of men who distort scripture to their own destruction, which explains what is happening with the homosexual issue. These religious scholars and teachers are really false teachers who are distorting the scriptures while trying to justify this abominable lifestyle. And, like those scholars and teachers, those who subscribe to those teachings are also condemning themselves to eternal destruction. One of those false teachings involve Ruth and Naomi, the account of which can be found in the bible in the Book of Ruth.

In order to survive a severe famine, a Jewish man named Elimelech had moved with his wife Naomi, and their two sons, Mahlon and Chilion, from Judah to Moab. Elimelech later died leaving Naomi a widowed single mother with two boys. Each boy grew up and married a Moabite woman. Their names were Ruth and Orpah. After about ten years, both of these men died, and Naomi's two Moabite daughters-in-law were left as widows. They developed a close relationship with Naomi over the years, perhaps becoming the daughters that she never had.

When her sons died, Naomi was in tremendous grief. After hearing that there was ample food in Judah, she had decided to return. All three of them began the trek towards Judah. But on the way, Naomi suggested that since both Ruth and Orpah were still young, they should go back to Moab and get on with their lives. The two young women, being attached to Naomi, refused to leave her. After a very tearful discussion that involved weeping and kissing, and a statement from Naomi acknowledging the existence of the Levirate Law of marriage,[123] Orpah decided that Naomi was right and said her final farewells and returned to Moab. Ruth however, adamantly refused to leave Naomi and made the now famous statement of commitment to Naomi:

And Ruth said, Intreat me not to leave thee, or to return from following after thee: for whither thou goest, I will go; and where thou lodgest, I will lodge: thy people shall be my people, and thy God my God: Where thou diest, will I die, and there will I be buried: the LORD do so to me, and more also, if ought but death part thee and me. Ruth 1:16-17

Religious proponents of homosexuality contend that these two women had a lesbian relationship. In their eyes, no one can be close if they are the same sex unless their relationship is a gay one. One of the first points that the story makes is effectively portrayed in the 18th verse where it says that Ruth was so "steadfastly minded to go with her," that is, return to Judah with Naomi, until she gave up trying to persuade Ruth to return home to her own people. Anything other understanding is simply false. The fact that Naomi suggested that Ruth meet Boaz who turned out to be Ruth's kinsman redeemer in Levirate marriage further proves it false that these women were lesbians.

On Ruth and Naomi, Helminiak says that since there is not much evidence about Ruth and Naomi, "it is impossible to say whether or not they shared a sexual relationship."[124]

I will correct Mr. Helminiak by averring that Ruth and Naomi had no sexual relationship at all, and the entire story as written proves that point without question.

Ruth and Naomi, as well as David and Jonathan, would be horribly insulted to hear the wicked things that are being circulated about them in some religious circles today by false teachers if they could know such things were being said about them.

The Prophet Daniel

In the book, <u>What the Bible *Really* Says About Homosexuality</u>, Helminiak on page 127 attempts to use Daniel 1:9 to imply to the reader that there may have been some kind of sexual relationship between Daniel and the prince of the eunuchs. The verse reads:

Now God had brought Daniel into favour and tender love with the prince of the eunuchs. Dan 1:9

To better understand this passage, one must first understand what a eunuch is. A eunuch is a castrated man whose primary job is to take care of a king's harem. Castration prevented this individual from sexual contact with the harem thus keeping the women safe from rape, molestation, or even an adulterous affair with him. At the same time, he was physically strong enough to meet the ladies' needs. According to Helminiak, some think that the eunuchs were not castrated men, but men who had sexual interest in men rather than in women. But history bears out evidence for the former position rather than his point of view which is pure speculation, a fact that even Helminiak himself admits by saying,

". . . there is some serious speculation that the servants at the court or the "eunuchs" in the ancient mid-East were not necessarily castrated men but rather men whose sexual interest was only for other men."[125]

So even Helminiak admits that it is only speculation and not based on any facts. The words "serious" and "speculation" should not be in the same sentence if *speculation* is just a guess. If it is a guess, then how can it be serious? False speculations are what causes religious proponents of homosexuality to erroneously think that any of the Godly men of the Old Testament could have engaged in an abominable relationship.

A word study of the "tender love" phrase shows us the meaning of original Hebrew word which is *uwlrachamiym*. Futher, The Theological Word Book of the Old Testament shows us that it is a "deep love," and it is used in Isaiah 49:15 of a mother's love for her baby. It can also be "a father's love," or the compassionate mercy that people can have towards others simply because they are human. It is also the feeling that is prompted by some for others who are weak or helpless.[126]

So the Hebrew word has nothing to do with either sex, or romance, but of tender compassion that a person has for another. The eunuch chief was troubled because Daniel, Hanniah, Azariah, and Mishael had refused to defile themselves with the king's food which consisted of things that were forbidden for them to eat. Because they had refused to eat, he knew that he would be held responsible if these young men showed up malnourished because it was his responsibility to take care of the young Hebrew men who were selected for their intelligence to help take care of Babylonian governmental matters.[127]

The bible states in Daniel 1:9 that God was the one who had initiated the special attention, compassion, and favor that the prince of the eunuchs had for Daniel which alone proves that the favor was for Daniel's advantage and protection and not for sex. The eunuch chief had such confidence in Daniel until he was willing to risk his own well-being and follow Daniel's suggestion concerning their rations rather than to take the king's orders on how they should be fed. Of course, God backed Daniel and his words and consequently, Daniel and company turned up healthier and better looking after just ten days than the others who had eaten the king's prescribed diet daily. The king had no idea that his orders had been ignored. They were ignored because God had given the prince of the eunuchs an attitude of more respect for Daniel than he had for the king. Therefore, with tender sympathetic compassion, he gave Daniel special treatment. Anyone who jumps to the conclusion that there was some kind of homosexuality between Daniel and the prince of the eunuchs does so with no facts at all.

Chapter Nine

SEX AND CHILDREN

⁂

*T*he most naïve people where sexuality about children is concerned are adults! To the uninformed, placing the word 'sexuality' in the same phrase with 'children' sounds like an oxymoron. Perhaps it should be, but unfortunately that is not the case. This chapter may be difficult for some because it contains information that is not easy to receive. It is not easy for me to write as it will be graphic and revealing about some of my own sensitive issues that I had as a child and growing teen. There is no attempt whatsoever to either glory or revel erotically in anything that I will share in this chapter because I am not proud of any of it. But while it is indeed shameful and sinful, I think that it is necessary for parents and professionals to consider because this kind of information is not always revealed in studies and research because of the nature of its sensitivity and shame. Children are more prone to hide rather than reveal these things. Most of the time, the experts will attempt to tie sexual behavior among children to some childhood familial relational problem such as dysfunction or past sexual abuse when that is not always the case. Some children, both boys and girls, simply learn to become sexually active early from some influence and they may belong to families that do not have those kinds of problems.

The information that will be presented in this chapter is difficult enough to the extent that there are those who will not be strong or mature enough to deal with it. Others, despite the fact that this information in no way condones child sexual activity, may become extremely uncomfortable and want to attack me in an effort to distance themselves from what is a very unpleasant subject because they themselves are not mature enough to deal with truth. But the truth must be revealed. Without such truth, a greater problem exists that is bigger than most people would expect that can have some serious consequences for many people for years to come.

Sexual Beings

The first truth that must be understood is this: children *are* sexual beings. We do not *become* sexual beings. We are <u>born</u> sexual beings because God made us that way. Children have the ability to experience sexual stimulation and even enjoy sexual intercourse. Sexuality does not need to develop in children because it is already there. Maturity, relational skills, life skills, discipline, good understanding, integrity, honesty, intelligence, knowledge, wisdom, good character, and morality are many of the attributes that need to be developed.

Children, despite being acutely aware of personal body parts, are generally not instinctively inclined towards sexual activity with others. Some of them may learn to masturbate early after discovering that genital rubbing or massaging produces pleasant sensations, but for the most part, children will ordinarily not instinctively pursue sexual partners.

However, that does not mean that children will absolutely not pursue sexual partners. Children can develop sex drives, and even have sexual addictions. Children as young as five or six can be drawn into a life of voluntary sexual promiscuity quite easily. All that is needed is some kind of sexual stimulus to awaken those latent desires, and that awakening in childhood can lead to a lifetime of problems and shame. I am sure that some people reading this fully understand that this is truth and are nodding in agreement because of their own personal experiences.

What many adults may not realize is that their children are not so eager to discuss their sexual proclivities with them, so their sexual behavior will largely remain undisclosed to those who are responsible for them, unless they are caught. Most of their sexual discussions will be with other children, especially those with similar interests, which is why it is important to teach children moral values as early as it is possible for them to understand—especially from a spiritual/biblical perspective.

My Story

When a very young boy becomes sexually active with no sense of morality, propriety, values, or boundaries, it can be disastrous. I know that first-hand. My first sexual relationship took place when I was about six years old—with a girl who was about five at the time. My aunt, with whom I lived at the time, would bring her over to be a playmate for me (that is what she told me in later years) since I was otherwise an only child when I lived with her. Soon after, we became sexually active and engaged in sex as often as we could until we were caught almost three years later. Over that time, my aunt was completely unaware of what was going on between us. Sometimes, some of our activities happened even while she was at home. What we did was not simply "harmless" experimentation. Here we can learn a very important lesson: never call sexual experimentation or exploration between children harmless, no matter what the experts say or believe. When "expertise" on human behaviors excludes God, the so-called expertise tends to only exacerbate bad behaviors, thus abetting the moral decay of children and our society.

When we were caught, my aunt had immediately assumed that it was I (because I was "the boy") who had influenced the girl into sexual activity and thus she blamed me for what we had done. At this point, we can destroy another myth of ignorance – that boys always lead girls to sexual activity. The truth is, I had known absolutely nothing about sex at the time. Our "relationship" began one day when she told me to look under the kitchen table and when I looked, she showed "herself" to me, and then asked me to do the same. I complied with what she wanted and can remember wanting to see "it" again. Now that had taken place while my aunt was in the house. Sometimes the subsequent "shows" continued to discreetly take place at the kitchen table even while auntie was nearby. This was possible because my aunt like many adults naively did not expect sexual behavior out of children so young. It is unfortunate that when such a possibility is sometimes suggested by adults who are more aware of the possibility, it is rebuffed with "You have a dirty mind!"

Our first intercourse occurred some time after the "shows" in a closet one afternoon while my aunt's husband was at home with us. He was busy outside in the backyard when the girl asked me to come into the closet, shut the door, and then she coaxed me to "put yours in mine like this." While I was afraid at first, that fear quickly changed into pleasure, and my childhood was changed (for the worst) right then and there. Now of course the worst did not happen immediately, and at the age of six I certainly did not know what bad could possibly come from doing something that felt so good. But sexual desire grew intensely inside of me from that point on. During my childhood, preteen and teen years, I had become completely sexually controlled and terribly immoral. I will not go into detail, but suffice it to say that it was not a nice journey. The only thing that saved me (pun intended) was when I received Jesus Christ into my life about one month after my eighteenth birthday.

God changed me completely from an immoral life-style that I have never returned to, and never want to return to. To say that I grew out of it would be an error. One cannot grow out of controlling immorality and perversion. One has to be delivered, and only the power of Jesus Christ can thoroughly effect such a deliverance.

Sexual Discovery

Now how do you think that this little five year-old girl had discovered what full sexual intercourse was and be able to lead me into it? The first thought that most people have is the typical catch-all reasoning for sexually active children—that she was prob-ably molested.. That reasoning exists because many people are naive about sexual sin, and its power to influence. They do not realize how the sexualized images and messages that bombard us daily adversely affect children. Remember that earlier, we said that children are sexual beings. If that is true, then chil-dren can be aroused just as adults are aroused, and by the same means that adults are aroused. In children, arousal will lead to desire, temptation, and finally experimentation. Experimentation becomes expe-rience which becomes the catalyst for more desire. And in a child, especially a boy, desire can grow with intensity with devastating results.

What had probably happened is that the girl had gotten hold of some pencil drawn porno-graphic pictures depicting various sexual positions. I can remember that these pictures were extremely well drawn and in perfect detail. Apparently, they had aroused her sexually and piqued her curiosity. Apparently after figuring out that it was something that she could do with me, she first began with simple acts of showing herself to me, and then wanting to "see" me. Finally, this behavior led to full sexual intercourse between us just like on the pictures.

One day she brought me to the drawer where the pictures had been and showed them to me for the first time. Along with the pictures were pornographic playing cards. Although I had lived in that house, I had never seen the pictures before and did not even know that they were there. They no doubt belonged to my aunt's husband. Apparently, she had found them while snooping around in the drawers in childish curiosity. After she showed them to me, we began trying out the various 'positions' that were depicted. We never engaged in the oral activity that was depicted because to us, that was repulsive and totally undesirable. Now if anyone had seen this otherwise normal looking six year-old boy and five-year-old girl, it would have never occurred to them what was going on between those two children on a regular basis over a 3 year period.

Secrets

The only time discussions of a sexual nature will generally take place between a child and an adult is when that discussion involves an adult who is responsible for the child, and who is giving that child some very important lessons on morality and virtue.

Otherwise, a young child and an adult are not going to have casual and openly explicit conversations about personal sexual things unless that child is very naïve and/or that adult has no boundaries and a perverse nature. One evening my wife and I, who had been involved in foster care for a number of years, had another foster parent couple at our home who was accompanied by their foster children. These were a boy and girl who were seven and six respectively. At some point, the little girl began to play childishly with me, and there was nothing wrong or inappropriate with the way she played with me, or I with her. We were all in the same room. But after that, she suddenly asked me a question that I did not understand so I had to ask her to repeat what she had asked. She repeated her question, but I still did not understand. The reason I did not understand is that my own adult naiveté had kicked in, and the way she asked the question was odd and not immediately understandable. But after about the second or third time I thought to myself, "Now I know that this child did not ask me what I think that she asked me." Even I who was not so pristine myself as a child was still somewhat naïve about children. I never expected her to ask me such a question. What made it difficult for me to understand her initially is that she had asked me "Do adults. . ." and then she completed the sentence by shaking her body. Now it was just a shake, and not anything that immediately appeared sexual in any manner, but the way she chose to ask the question threw me for a loop. There was nothing that I had done to provoke her curiosity and when she asked the question, it was not loud enough for the others to hear. She finally cleared up her question by asking "Do adults, you know, *do it—sex*?" Now I understood what she was asking me! I then gently told her that her question was very inappropriate and that she should never ask any adult a question like that. Afterward, I told her foster mom what she had asked so that she could further instruct her. Obviously this child was already sexually aware, and who knows how experienced. She knew what sex was, and then was asking me if adults participated in that activity, implying that in her mind, she understood that children engaged in sex, but she was wondering if adults did the same. It seems reasonable that she was never molested by an adult since she did not know whether adults "did it" or not. Through her naiveté, she had committed a rare breach of the unspoken rule that children do not normally discuss sex in a casual manner with adults.

Our over-sexualized culture does not teach children that sex is wrong outside of marriage, or that it is a private activity. Instead, our society voyeuristically depicts sex as an indiscriminate recreation as if there are no boundaries at all. Had that little girl been with a child predator instead of me, her question could have opened the door for that person to take advantage of her. Nevertheless, it is because of the otherwise aforementioned secrecy that adults are not usually aware of just how sexually active children may be. If an adult would query their young son or daughter as to sexual experience, and let's say that the child was indeed sexually experienced, do you think that the child is going to say, "Yes mom (or dad). Me and [blank] do it all the time?" I don't think so either.

So it is imperative for responsible adults to be watchful guardians, while teaching children very early about moral issues, and that sex belongs in marriage. At this point, we can appreciate the fact that God wanted the parents of His people to instruct their children about His laws of sexuality. For us, such teaching can at first begin with truths that are simple for them to comprehend, such as the fact that they should not show their private parts to anyone, nor should they ask or want to see anyone else's private parts, and that when people do those kinds of things, God is greatly disappointed. After all, constant gawking at nakedness is the first broken barrier toward inappropriate sexual activity.

Consequences of Sexual Children

Now here is another truth that must be exposed to help remove some of the ignorance that pervades the adult world. In today's climate, adults may be involved sexually with children, and then someone may ask how in the world can they do that and what does a grown person see in a little child? The answer will open some eyes. First of all, what could a seven year old boy see in a six year old girl? Well, once he has had sex with her, that's not a difficult question to answer. After that, every little girl—even infants— can become a possible sexual conquest to him. Once a very young boy has experienced sex, it is potentially dangerous for him and others around him because he has no concept of discretion or boundaries. For him, a girl is a girl and sex is sex. At that point, sex becomes the desirable goal with almost every and any girl he encounters. And in his pursuit, he may not use the word 'sex,' but rather the most common description of what he wants from a girl would be his description of choice, a word beginning with the 16th letter of the alphabet. He learns lust without the virtues of love and commitment. When he turns ten, seven year old girls will still be sex objects to him. As he gets older, while he may prefer older girls, if he should come to a place where frequent sexual encounters are rare which is the norm for children and teens, it can cause him to become opportunistic when he comes in contact with younger females in unsupervised situations. Because the moral boundary had been crossed earlier in his life, he can grow up still visualizing very young girls only as sex objects. It is very easy for a boy to grow all the way up into manhood still seeing six year old girls as sex objects, especially if his first sexual experiences were with six year old girls when he was the same age. This may not be true of all men who had early sexual experiences in childhood, but it is one main reason why grown men may pursue little girls sexually. What you have is a little boy who learned sex without first developing a sense of boundaries and propriety. After he is grown and develops that sense somewhat, it becomes over-ridden by desire and fantasy which drives his actions. In the meantime, our society relentlessly promotes ungodly sexual values to young boys, not realizing the immoral damage that is being done to them. Then we are shocked and angered when in their future they act out on the liberal immorality that they have learned. While this may be shocking to some, I'm expressing truth that I know some people are afraid to express, and that research may not uncover. Now, it is time to get into some of the reasons for children's sexual indulgences.

Other Reasons Children Become Prematurely Sexualized

As we learned earlier, children are sexual beings who can be aroused sexually by sights and images. What aroused the little girl in my experience were pictures she found in a day where sexual images were not as prevalent as they are now. A healthy young boy can be aroused in a few seconds by any sight, sound, or thought that vaguely appears sexual. And in today's sexual climate, any child can easily become sexualized by this generation that eats, sleeps, and breathes sex all day long, in books, magazines, novels, sitcoms, movies, commercials, articles, documentaries, wildlife programs, music, hip hop, general conversation, personal video libraries, internet video services, cell phone videos, DVDs, video games, news reports, porn on and off the internet, and other internet sources. If these influences existed when I was a child, it would have been far more difficult for me because I would have had more to trap me thanks to the endless stream of images and materials produced by adults (and even children) today. Only time will tell how many children, both boys and girls, have been liberally sexualized by the flood of sexual material that is now pervading the globe freely with little or no restraints.

In the 1950s and before, those generations of adults tried their best keep their raw material away from the eyes and ears of children. Even then, we were still able to see some of the porn that existed whether in magazines, or the occasional pictures that could be found on the ground or in someone's trash, underneath a car seat, hidden in a drawer or closet, or that a student may have obtained somehow and brought to school.

For today's child, prime time television may show a man and a woman writhing under sheets quite easily and although they may be covered, it is no secret what they are doing. Such images are extremely arousing for any young boy and especially one who has already discovered intercourse. VHS tapes and DVDs, are readily available in many private home libraries which children may have access to. Cable and satellite provide ample opportunities to see real live flesh action when preview week comes around, or when a movie shown is not rated that would otherwise be blocked out, or when a premium channel otherwise blocked is somehow "open" so that its programming content becomes viewable to anyone who happens to channel surf to it. I have had several experiences where I was simply changing channels and happened across a premium channel that I did not subscribe to that was "open" for viewing. The sexual content was in full view and left nothing to the imagination. I have always completely blocked certain channels so that they could not be accessed in my home at all, especially by my children.

The overexposure of sexual programming today is due to the moral deficits in today's producers. Perhaps when they were children, they had no moral boundaries and were somehow exposed to heavy sexual content, or they were taught moral values and have simply forsaken or rejected them just as biblical Israel rejected God's law. When people question why certain things are considered wrong and inappropriate, rejection of those values follow if the answer is deemed inadequate. Questioning of moral standards happen when people no longer subscribe to the higher standard that God has left for us to follow. When degenerate sexual immorality is questioned they may reject the challenge by asking, "What's the big deal?" Therefore, they do not care that children are exposed to inappropriate sexual content. They are only interested in the monetary profits that can be earned as a result of such content. They contend that parents should monitor what children watch. But that is not always possible. The truth is that all of society should take on the responsibility of not allowing children to be exposed to inappropriate content because it can lead to unfortunate consequences when sexual arousal is awakened in them. Besides, one parent can be extremely careful with the content his or her child is exposed to, and another parent can be negligent. The child of a negligent adult can easily expose another child to inappropriate content who in turn can expose a non-negligent parent's child through the interaction of children in school. Children can also expose other children through inappropriate conversation, personal experiences, various types of sexual material, and sexual behavior, or inappropriate touching, play, or jokes.

When sexuality is awakened in young males, dire consequences can be the result. They can learn to become violent, sneaky, or manipulative for the purpose of sexual gratification, due to the increasing desire growing within them. Another bad but well-kept secret is that of young boys who get up in the middle of the night when everyone else is asleep to gratify themselves on the young females who may be present in the home. If the children who are accosted are deep sleepers, it may never be known to them that this has been done to them. If siblings or other children are willing participants, then parents may never know all that has been going on in the home.

Two More Stories

I will tell two not so very nice stories from my childhood. A friend of mine and I were walking together one day and I do not remember where we were coming from but we were very close to home. I guess that we were about 11 or 12 years old or so at the time. As we passed an apartment building, a young girl who could have been about seven or eight years of age was playing on a cinder-block fence that ran along behind her apartment building. When I saw her, a very stupid thought came into my mind to go and grab her and rape her. Impulsively, I was ready to try it. Today as a grown, mature and Godly adult,

I can see how really stupid that thought was. But as a young, sex-driven, immature and naïve boy with no boundaries, I had no idea of how dumb it was to even consider such a thought. At that very moment, the girl's mother had called her name from inside her apartment and told her to come inside. Then my friend made a startling comment. He said, "It's a good thing that her mother called her inside because I was going to go and grab her and rape her!" Astonished upon hearing that, I said, "Me, too!" Here we were — two boys, walking down the street together who had received the very same impulse at the very same time to do the very same thing. After coming to Christ, and looking back on it, I realized that the influence of devils regarding evil, especially where temptation is concerned, is real. No doubt a rape would have never occurred and we probably would have been arrested and charged — if not killed first by the girl's mom. The girl's dad could have been home as well, and he would have not taken too kindly to us either for attacking his daughter and we might have wished we were dead! I consider it a blessing to this day that the girl was called in and nothing ever happened.

I am not at all proud of any of these confessions. I am only sharing them to inform and warn others of the potential dangers of sexual stimulation, sexual experience, sexual exposure, and the sexual influence of children. Boys should be taught that sex belongs in marriage only and is a precious gift to be shared only between him and his wife in a committed, loving relationship, and that it should be reserved for such. Girls should be taught the same thing concerning sex and marriage and that they should expect to be respected as future wife-lovers rather than sex objects for momentary personal gratification. Both boys and girls should also be taught early on that despite the momentary pleasure, they can suffer from severe physical, emotional, and behavioral problems from childhood sexual encounters.

Streetwalker

Here is another not so nice confession. Somewhere between the ages of 12 and 14, I walked the streets after dark, compelled by a strong wanton desire, looking for some lone girl to rape. In my mind, I was going to choose one who was at least weaker and smaller than myself who may have been on an errand for her parents, and in some isolated place. I prowled around like that several times without any success at all. Years after Jesus came into my life, I looked back on those days and rejoiced in the fact that I was never successful. Therefore, I cannot over-emphasize the reason children must be taught God's will where sex is concerned. Without that teaching, the sinful nature of human beings will certainly take what God meant to be a beautiful and loving experience and turn it into something regretfully ugly – an ugliness that can begin in very early childhood.

Good Reasons to Avoid Fornication

The bible teaches us to avoid fornication.[128] Such teaching is very important, not only from the standpoint of the avoidance of personal sin, but it is important because of the examples that it presents to children. The nature of children is selfish as it is, making it necessary to teach them to consider others. In males, that selfishness is only exacerbated to the point where gratification becomes the only goal and its consequences are no longer a factor. As a result, diseases spread, children are neglected, wives and girlfriends are abandoned and cheated on, women and girls are raped, and they are also used and taken advantage of becoming nothing more than toys that are played with for a little while, and then discarded. God did not intend for that to happen when He made the woman for the man.

The openly sexualized messages that are being sent in today's media are only creating problems for the sake of financial profiteering. When these problems begin festering in children, they will haunt that generation's future.

Hypocrisy

Our society only pretends to not want children sexualized. On the one hand, you hear people saying that children shouldn't see or hear some things, and on the other hand, you see the things that children shouldn't hear or see being exposed to them in the name of "free speech" and promoted without responsibility. Many of today's television producers are perverts. They know children may be watching, but they do not care. Once, during a Monday Night Football game during the 2004 season, a commercial was shown that depicted a man waiting in a meeting room where a cell phone rang that sat on a conference table. The man proceeded to answer it and the phone's display showed a woman suppposedly doing a very sensual strip tease for her husband. After the woman was unclothed down to her bra and panties, his co-worker, the owner of the phone walked in, and the man hurriedly turned the phone off and set it back on the table and said to his co-worker, "Your wife called." My issue with the commercial is that there were no doubt young children watching this commercial because it was aired in prime-time during a national sports telecast. The advertiser, the producers of the game, the NFL, and the station airing the telecast all made a poor decision. Such a commercial can imply to children (especially to little girls) that public sexual and sensual display is okay—especially if adults are promoting it, and that this is what males and society expect out of them. I have one question to present to everyone with respect to that commercial: let's say that this commercial had never publicly aired before. Would those same individuals responsible for that commercial approve if any adult had privately shown that very same sequence to any of their ten-year-old relatives?

Some of the film industry's producers might even star children into overtly sexualized scripts. Hollywood has produced movies depicting girls or boys racing each other to lose their virginity or children in very obvious sexual situations and dialogue, young teens simulating sex, and even adults supposedly giving children their first sexual experi-

217

ence such as in the 1981 movie *Private Lessons* in which a voluptuous maid gives a fifteen-year-old boy his first "lessons."[129] These types of movies tend to make sex look like something that is only fun with no responsibility or consequences at all which is very misleading to children. Anytime a script is produced, sex can be written to look like good fun only with no consequences and where everybody lives "happily ever after." But real-life does not follow movie scripts, and the real results can be devastating, which is the main reason God intended for sex to be confined to the committed marital relationship.

One such disturbing movie is the one entitled *L.I.E.* The letters stand for Long Island Expressway and it is about a man who craved homosexual relationships with teen boys. The movie opens with a very disturbing scene as a conversation between four boys. One of the boys brags that he has had sex with his 11 year old sister using the "f" word to describe his conquest. When the other boys act as if they don't believe him, he bets them $20 to prove it and invites them to come and watch. As a result, one of the other boys wistfully exclaims, "I wish I had a sister!"[130] At the time of this writing (2005), that scene was the main promo trailer and could be easily viewed on the internet. A very impressionable and wanton boy watching that scene could be encouraged to try and coax his younger sister into having sex with him simply "to see what it feels like." Perhaps he would not have ever thought of doing that before seeing the movie. The scene seems to approve of the incestuous behavior despite their discussion about birth deformities of children conceived by siblings. So while one part of our society claims to want to "protect" children from sexual behavior, in a contrary fashion another part promotes illicit messages to and about them indiscriminately that can easily influence them to become sexual with their friends, siblings, or other close relatives.

It may be surprising to learn that sibling sex is more prevalent than one would think. I do not remember the source, but I once read an article that revealed that incestuous sexual relationships are easier to come by between a brother and a sister because a sister may not be as quick to resist the advances of a brother (and vice versa) than a non-sibling because of the close familiarity. When the sister is younger, she may look up to her brother and as a result be eager to please him in any way. As a matter of fact, because of the internet and exchange of anonymous information, and because this generation is less moral and more ungodly, more siblings are admitting to sexual relationships, having children together, and even living as married couples. So such a movie can easily encourage incest, by putting ideas into a boy's head that he might not have considered before, which can have a devastating impact on himself, his family, and the emotional and moral development of his young sister. Yet it appears that the movie industry is stubbornly perverted because it resists objections to the messages that it promotes in the name of entertainment that brings profit.

My Life as a Dog[131] is another movie that also toys with sex and children. The movie has an early scene with a little girl laying down underneath a short railroad trestle attempting to coax the little boy to "come on." The scene shows only the legs of the girl (who is about 9 or10 in the movie) laying down with the top portion of her body hidden, attempting to get the boy to remove his clothes and lay on top of her. The boy is hesitant and stalls until the oncoming train startles him, causing him to jump, and he somehow ends up falling on top of her. But her father comes at that moment, and catches him in that position and asks, "What the h… are you doing to my daughter?" so the scene ends at that point. The clear and blatant sexual overtones between pre-adolescent children can only serve to awaken the sexual natures of children who are watching and tempt them by arousal to engage in practices that can cause them to be sorry later. The movie has another scene before that in which the boy is coerced to put his penis into a bottle where it gets stuck while the other children present – boys and girls – laugh at him.

Video Games and The Internet

There is a game made for the Xbox® game called Grand Theft Auto® in which there are some extremely graphic sex scenes that children can watch while playing. The scenes are player "rewards" for certain accomplishments.

The internet is still another medium that promotes and encourages sexual behavior among children. Personal video websitess can show all sorts of sexual activity that can easily be accessed by children. In some cases the videos may feature the children themselves. I recently saw a video where a girl of about 8 years old was dancing with a boy of about 7. It was a very sexual, steamy, racy, vulgar, erotic fast-pace no-holds-barred dance where it looked as if the girl was trying her best to stimulate and sexually gratify her dancing partner while other children stood around and watched in delight. Still another video featured a dancing group of five 8 year-old girls dancing to Beyonces's song entitled "Single Ladies" in a very vulgar and sexual manner. They were wearing very tight hot pants with bare midriffs. The dance was replete with squatting and legs gapped wide open along with pelveses thrusting backward and forward towards the audience. Parents of the little girls approved the performance, which while very vulgar at best, provoked an outcry from concerned citizens. Yet that kind of dancing has been going on for years among very young girls in the black community with parental encouragement thanks to the hip-hop phenomenon.

Still again the modeling industry also sends messages that reek of hypocrisy. As of this revisional writing, 10 year old French model Thylane Blondeau who is quickly becoming a very popular but controversial model was presented in a picture in which she is topless and sitting on a bed with a topless young boy who is standing nearby on the same bed and holding a pillow. It is alleged by bloggers that a caption over the photo on her website read: "SHE'S NOT WEARING A TOP BECAUSE SHE DIDN'T THINK IT WOULD OFFEND ANYONE shoot me."[132] If in fact that was her reasoning for being photographed topless, the question that immediately comes to mind is, what kind of world has this become wherein a photo of a topless 10 year old girl can be displayed internationally along with a topless boy, and not be considered offensive but perhaps enjoyed by everyone? Is our world slowly becoming that callous? She has also modeled in several other photos topless, and all of them can easily be viewed on the internet.

Because of human departure from true Godly and Christlike standards, people in our society do not know how to be an appropriate example for children where sexual matters are concerned. The result is that children can become exploited sexually, sexualized, and even become uncontrollably sexually active. The message from society to them on the one hand is the implication that sex is only fun (without responsibility) and that they should "use protection." Then on the other hand, they are exploited as sexual teases and bombarded with sexual entertainment for profit. The consequences for lack of Godly moral influence is fornication, adultery, rape, murder involving sexual acts, prostitution, child molestation, bestiality, sexual promiscuity in the media and entertainment, broken marriages, broken homes and broken families, diseases, unwanted pregnancies, adolescent and pre-adolescent pregnancies, abortion, sexual hypocrisy in the world, and young boys who learn to use and abuse children sexually. Then they grow up as men and continue to do the same. Even women can become users and abusers and these abuses together bring a whole host of other ills that create unnecessary burdens upon our entire society. All that sounds a lot like Sodom!

God's Law vs. Man's Law

Since our society has such an unscriptural view of sex, this writing is designed to introduce God's righteousness and God's judgment where matters of sex is concerned. We have consent laws that attempt to govern sexual activity between individuals when one of them is at least three years older than the other one when that one is under the age of majority, even if the activity was initiated by that younger person. The law considers the act *abuse,* and even *rape*. But those terms can be misleading. Don't forget that children are secretive where their own willful sexual activity is concerned, and their behaviors may not be known unless they are somehow caught. Personally, I believe that the law ought to make <u>all</u> sexual activity outside of marriage illegal, which would be in line with the way that God wants it. But men who make laws today are more afraid to line up with their Creator who can punish eternally and with severe judgment, and are less afraid to line up with other men, whose ability to simply vocally object is woefully limited to just that by comparison.

When one child within the same age range is caught consensually with another, there is absolutely no legal jurisdiction over their actions whatsoever. For example, if a twelve-year-old boy is caught with a ten-year-old girl. And both were willing participants. There are no legal penalties for either of them, and depending upon the parents, they may or may not take any familial disciplinary action. But if the girl is seven with the same boy, the boy could face rape charges, even if the girl was a willing participant. If a ten-year-old girl is a willing participant and is caught with a fifteen-year-old boy, now he could be charged with rape. If instead the girl is fourteen, then no one can be charged, although the act is the same. But if that same fourteen-year-old girl is caught with a ten-year-old boy, now she faces charges, regardless of his wilful participation. But if the same ten-year-old boy is caught with a six year old girl in the same kind of situation such as I encountered when I was seven, *he* faces charges—even though she would have coerced him! That's kind of like when my aunt beat and blamed me more because she presumably thought that I was responsible for the relationship that the girl and I had. In all the above scenarios, we are talking about people who willfully all commited the very same act and were all guilty in the sight of God of the same sin – fornication, but are charged or are not legally charged dependent upon the situation.

There is plenty wrong with this picture, at least where man is concerned. In each hypothetical situation, we have willing participants, but the law is only prosecuting the oldest, as if the youngest is completely innocent, even if the youngest could be similarly charged under different circumstances. Yet, people find fault with God's law with regards to rape and its solution in the Torah that was previously discussed in an earlier chapter. If righteousness is properly taught to children, many of the consequential problems experienced in our society can be avoided.

God's law does not work like man's law. He sees all the participants as equally guilty of sin, regardless of their ages. God judges the heart, and the willingness of a child to behave sexually makes him or her guilty before God, whether or not they fully know or understand that such actions are sinful, and regardless of how old or young they are. In Israel it was necessary for parents to teach God's statutes to their children. Violation of His statutes is sin. If the child did not know, it was because the parents did not teach the child and they too would've been held responsible for that neglect. Regardless, the child is still personally responsible for his or her sin before God.

While the law of God required the girl to receive an immediate consequence, the male who may have accosted her was not at all guiltless before God. God knew however, that teaching them while they were children and instilling in them what He required would help to make a difference where prevention of such acts was concerned, especially when they want to obey His commandments.

Why Children can be Guilty of Sexual Sin

Now here is the reason that such action brings automatic guilt in consenting children. Remember, according the apostle Paul in the book of Romans 1, there are some things that we know intrinsically, because God has revealed that to us. We naturally have some concepts and understanding of right and wrong. Here is one test that can decide whether a person knows what they are doing is wrong: when one child willingly decides to engage sexually with another, where is it accomplished? Is it done openly and freely discussed, or is it done in a secluded place and kept secret? For example, when the girl and I had our first sexual experience, it was in a closet and the door was closed and we kept our activity hidden from the adults. Those actions prove that we knew that what we were doing was wrong, even if we did not fully understand why. When children hide their actions, it is because they know that they can get "in trouble" if they are discovered.

One of the most self-contradictory concepts in law that exists on the books is the "consent" law where the idea is that children cannot legally consent to sex. I beg to differ. I don't like the word *consent* as it is because they *can* and do consent to sex. Now they may not consent with society's or legal permission, or with mature information, but they can and do consent on their own volition, based on the meaning of the word which means to permit, agree, comply or yield. If a child can agree to sex, that is consent. If we are saying that it is not legal for that child to 'consent,' then the child should be legally dealt with in some manner as well. They may not consent with knowledge, maturity, or with the proper understanding of the ramifications of their actions (sometimes that is true of many adults!) but yet, they can and do consent. I would prefer to say that they cannot make *informed,* or even *legal* consent, which makes much more sense.

However, children do consent to sex and God knows that and He doesn't give a hoot about our law when He makes His judgments. I just read a story of a girl who at age 11 was angry with her father for not being "there for her," so she retaliated against him by accusing him of sexually molesting her, resulting in his being jailed. After being jailed for about 10 of a 15 year sentence, she remorsefully recanted her accusation and he was released. However, she admitted to having been involved in sexual activities since the *second grade.* If her admitted sexual behavior was not "consent," then what is? It is incumbent upon us to tell children the truth when they become aware of sexual issues, or when they are old enough to understand, that sexual intercourse belongs in marriage, and that contrary lifestyles, God will judge. Man may not want to condemn children in some "consent" scenarios, but unfortunately, God will condemn all of their consensual sexual behavior!

Because children can make a conscious decision to willfully engage in sexual intercourse, sometimes it is the child who may initiate sex, even with an adult. This does happen. Yet, in our law, only the adult will be prosecuted. But God *will* judge the child also, because God knows that the child does indeed understand that their involvement in sex is not right. This is evident when someone touches a child inappropriately. Instinctively, the child knows that the contact is wrong and despite any pleasurable sensations, he or she will also acknowledge that there was something about the touch that alerted them that it was something that should not have been done, even if the person doing the touching claims to have been "just playing."

My purpose here is to show how God fully judges what man may judge incompletely. Unfortunately, people do not understand God's purpose behind sex. God will <u>never</u> sanction sex between *adults* who are not married to each other. Yet, God will sanction sex between any properly married couple, even if one of them is under the age of majority. Therefore, if a thirty-year-old man and woman engage sexually, and they are not married, they have committed the sin of fornication where God is concerned. But if a thirty-year-old man and a fourteen-year-old girl are married and they engage sexually, they have not sinned before God. That is true whether you advocate such a marital relationship or not. The bible teaches,

> *Marriage is to be held in honor among all, and the marriage bed is to be undefiled; for fornicators and adulterers God will judge.* Hebrews 13:4 NASU

Almost everyone will agree that such a girl as in the above example is too young for marriage which is a relationship that requires maturity (although there are many adults who should be considered too immature for marriage!). However, some will marry very young anyway, and sometimes to older people. That has happened ever since there was a world, and that is a subject the bible has been completely silent about. But if we believe that a teen girl is too young for marriage, then why does our society allow them to be sexual or sexualized? Why have we allowed organizations to pass out condoms to them and encourage them to use them under the guise of "safe sex" when premarital and promiscuous sex are known to cause serious problems? Why are some parents allowing their pre-adolescent girls to dress as "prostitots"?[133] Why do some parents dress their young girls in clothing that says "Baby", "Luscious", or "Cute" written across their bottoms? Does anyone realize that attention has to be called to a young girl's bottoms in order to read some of those messages? Another sad testimony to this generation is that nowadays, as soon as some girls grow breasts, they begin to wear low-cut clothing to show their cleavages. This is true even of many church girls who consider themselves Christians. That also includes the very short skirts and shorts, exposed belly buttons and mid-drifts, low-cut jeans and slacks that reveal undergarments and rear cleavages. There are some who may think that I am attempting to make up rules that everyone should live by but that is not so. The apostle Paul wrote under the inspiration of the Holy Spirit when he wrote,

In like manner also, that women adorn themselves in modest apparel, with shamefacedness and sobriety. . . 1 Timothy 2:9

The conflicting hypocritical messages are wrong. If we do not like the idea of a girl getting married at thirteen, then we should not allow society to turn them into sex objects at ten.

Another Sexual Little Girl

When my oldest son was about nine years old and showed curiosity about where babies come from, I sat down with him and explained to him about how God made us and the entire reproductive process which grossed him out. I then opened the Word of God and explained to him about God's blessing of man and woman to be fruitful and multiply, the fact that sex belonged in marriage, and that outside of marriage it is called the sin of fornication, and that the bible teaches that God will punish fornicators. I did this carefully using various verses from scripture and told him as much as his curious little mind could handle. He understood with no problem.

At that time, he was attending a private Catholic school, which my wife and I had chosen for its academics. Some time later, he related to me the following conversation he had with one of his little female classmates. He said: "Daddy!" Guess what this girl told me? She asked me if I had ever had sex before and I told her 'Girl, that's for married people.' And guess what she said to me? She said 'Boy, you don't know what you're missing!'"

Now this came from the mouth of a girl who was probably the same age as my son to whom I had taught proper sexual values. It sounded as if this girl had already experienced sexual intercourse based on her statement, and was probably attempting to encourage my son into experiencing it too, perhaps with her. I'm willing to bet the rent that her parents never knew her personal opinion about how good sex felt. Could this have been her attempt at "consent" with my son? My instruction not only prevented him from being corrupted at a very early age as was I, but at least it prevented my son from giving in to a naïve little girl, and it also kept him from dealing with the depths of what I had experienced growing up. Since I had instructed him, he attempted to set the little girl straight, rather than give in to her and unbeknowingst to him adversely affect his life. And who knows how many *unconsenting* little girls might have been later saved from sexual trauma as a result? In his mind, God would not be pleased, and he did not want to displease God, which is the effect that the word of God can have on a child. As he grew into manhood, he met a Christian girl and did not have sex with her at all during their six year courtship whom he married as a virgin. When a parent takes time to teach sexual issues to a child from the word of God, that is the good that can happen.

Anyone who thinks that children cannot be sexual or will not initiate sex with anyone at all, does not know the potential sexual nature of children, and are themselves very naïve.

Chapter Ten

SEX AND JUDGMENT

❧

Now concerning the things whereof ye wrote unto me: It is good for a man not to touch a woman. Nevertheless, to avoid fornication, let every man have his own wife, and let every woman have her own husband. 1 Corinthians 7:1-2

Marriage is honourable in all, and the bed undefiled: but whoremongers and adulterers God will judge. Hebrews 13:4

*T*he word of God has been straightforward about sinful sexual behavior and its consequences. One point brought out earlier in this book cannot be over-emphasized: *God is merciful.* People are allowed to continue in sin only because God does not want to destroy anyone. Rather, God wants repentance. When God sends a warning, He wants people to heed the warning so that He will not have to bring His final judgment upon them. Sometimes His judgments are merely corrective measures equivalent to spankings that are simply designed to get our attention, so as a result they are not always immediately fatal. Some judgments are precursors to more severe judgments. Failure to heed the scriptural warning to avoid fornication and follow the will of God where sex is concerned will only bring on more judgments.

What kind of judgments are we talking about? Let's go back to Romans 1.

For the wrath of God is revealed from heaven against all ungodliness and unrighteousness of men, who hold the truth in unrighteousness; Romans 1:18

Those who *suppress* or 'hold down' the truth and continue to live in unrighteousness will incur God's wrath. Still further, Paul writes,

And likewise also the men, leaving the natural use of the woman, burned in their lust one toward another; men with men working that which is unseemly, and receiving in themselves that recompence of their error which was meet. And even as they did not like to retain God in their knowledge, God gave them over to a reprobate mind, to do those things which are not convenient; being filled with all unrighteousness, fornication, wickedness, covetousness, maliciousness; full of

*envy, murder, debate, deceit, malignity; whis-
perers, backbiters, haters of God, despiteful,
proud, boasters, inventors of evil things, disobedient to parents, without understanding,
covenant-breakers, without natural affection, implacable, unmerciful: who knowing
the judgment of God, that they which commit
such things are worthy of death, not only do
the same, but have pleasure in them that do
them. Romans 1:27-32*

The Holy Spirit is teaching us through the
Apostle Paul that those who commit all the listed acts
(including homosexuality) will eventually receive
the penalty they deserve as a result of that kind of
living. God's judgment is incurred only when people
who commit those things fail to repent. Paul clarifies
what reprobation is—that it is a list of things and not
just homosexuality, and that all of those behaviors
all fall under the same category and are worthy of
the judgment of death. All of those things in Paul's
list are sinful behaviors of depraved and reprobate
minds, and remember—the wages of sin is death.

*Flee fornication. Every sin that a man doeth
is without the body; but he that committeth
fornication sinneth against his own body.
1 Corinthians 6:18*

To the Christian, Paul writes that we must run
from immorality because our bodies are for the service of the Lord. Here Paul teaches us what believers

are *not* to do with their bodies. He goes on in the context saying that when you are a believer, your body belongs to God and that it no longer belongs to you and He does not want you to take what belongs to Him and use it for immorality of any kind.

Or do you not know that the unrighteous will not inherit the kingdom of God? Do not be deceived; neither fornicators, nor idolaters, nor adulterers, nor effeminate, nor homosexuals, nor thieves, nor the covetous, nor drunkards, nor revilers, nor swindlers, will inherit the kingdom of God. Such were some of you; but you were washed, but you were sanctified, but you were justified in the name of the Lord Jesus Christ and in the Spirit of our God. 1 Corinthians 6:9-11 NASU

You just read the main danger of those lifestyles: the loss of eternal life. One must ask whether *any* immoral or other sinful lifestyle is worth that. To sacrifice the eternal for the temporal is not very wise. God wants us all to be saved, but immorality will definitely prevent salvation and instead bring about eternal damnation.

But the fearful, and unbelieving, and the abominable, and murderers, and whoremongers, and sorcerers, and idolaters, and all liars, shall have their part in the lake which burneth with fire and brimstone: which is the second death. Revelation 21:8

In the passage, "whoremongers" refer to fornicators, and you can see that the abominable are not left out, which includes all abominable acts such as idolatry or homosexuality. We have learned so far that homosexuality is fornication too, and it is also abomination. Religious groups and individuals who teach otherwise will do all who listen to them a terrible disservice where eternal life is concerned because they are certainly not teaching the word of God. Sadly, many otherwise intelligent people can read plain scripture and yet ascribe to it a meaning other than what it is plainly saying, or suddenly pretend to not understand its plain meaning. Such suppression of truth will certainly lead to the eternal damnation of countless millions of precious souls whom Jesus loved and died for. The reason is that the love of immoral desire in some people, which is the main drive of homosexuality, is far greater than any love for God, and that is as abominable as idolatry. The love for homosexuality and idolatry is also greater than the love for God's commandments. Thus, the reason for God's disgust. Idolatry and homosexuality take the hearts of the people He loves away from Him through their sin.

Homosexuals and proponents of homosexuality—religious or otherwise—commit a great error when they falsely and ignorantly accuse this message as one of hatred. Paul, in 1 Corinthians 6:9-11, listed the reasons people will not enter into the kingdom of heaven as being due to certain lifestyles, and then reminded the Corinthian believers that they too once lived like that. All of us who are saved today were once somewhere on that list and were headed to the same burning lake of fire until we came to Jesus and were born again. There is no way that any of us can hate any sinner and please God, no matter what that sinner has done. Now granted, there are a few ignorant people associated with the church who do not have a full concept of God's love, and will promote such awful and ungodly messages such as "God hates fags." One can find ignorance in any group or organization of people and the Christian church is no exception. But there is not one of us who can look down on any sinner because we are not saved by our own goodness, but only by the grace of God. And but for His grace through Jesus Christ, we who are now Christians would also face eternal damnation in the lake of fire. Every one of us.

Chapter Eleven

HOMOSEXUALS AND GOD'S LOVE

One of the most misunderstood concepts of about God is His love. Not many people are going to argue against God's love for us. The message of the bible is filled with God's love. For example:

The one who does not love does not know God, for God is love. 1 John 4:8 NASU

"For God so loved the world, that He gave His only begotten Son, that whoever believes in Him shall not perish, but have eternal life. John 3:16 NASU

Without question, God is love. That God loves us does not mean that He will tolerate everything that we may do which is the main mistake that people make when referring to the love of God.

Proper Understanding of God's Love

Here is the proper way to understand God's love. First of all, we must understand that God does not owe any of us anything, and that none of us deserves anything from God but eternal damnation. That is what the Torah teaches. It plainly states that there is not anyone who is initially deemed as righteous by the law of God.[134] So actually, every one of us are born unworthy of eternal life from day one. As we said in chapter 2, the standard which God will judge all of us by is His Torah (law) because it shows us what sin is according to Romans 7:7. Our problem is that none of us can satisfy all of the Torah's righteous demands no matter what we do. If the wages of sin is death according to Romans 6:23, and we are all guilty of sin according to Romans 3:23, and we are all unrighteous according to Romans 3:10, and we cannot be justified even if we could satisfy all of the commandments according to Romans 3:20, then through the law, there is no chance for salvation for any of us. But because God loves us, He sent his Son to take our place in death, suffering the penalty of sin for us in our stead. In doing so, the shed blood of Jesus atones, that is, covers our sin for us before God. Although we still cannot completely measure up to God's righteous standards, the blood of Christ covers for our shortcomings which demonstrates the love of God. The Apostle Paul wrote:

> *For while we were still helpless, at the right time Christ died for the ungodly. For one*

will hardly die for a righteous man; though perhaps for the good man someone would dare even to die. But God demonstrates His own love toward us, in that while we were yet sinners, Christ died for us. Much more then, having now been justified by His blood, we shall be saved from the wrath of God through Him. For if while we were enemies we were reconciled to God through the death of His Son, much more, having been reconciled, we shall be saved by His life. And not only this, but we also exult in God through our Lord Jesus Christ, through whom we have now received the reconciliation. Romans 5:6-11 NASU

Let's understand what Paul has said. He related from his own experience when he had vehemently fought against the church of God and was on his way to Damascus in an attempt to put any believer in Christ into prison where he was met supernaturally by Jesus instead. Although he had fought against the purposes of God, God still loved him. Although he fought against God's Son, God still loved him. Although he fought against God's people, still God loved him. Now God never once condoned anything he did and Paul was certainly in danger of God's judgment, but God loved him anyway. Keep in mind that Paul was also religious and erroneously thought that he was doing what God would want him to do. Paul could have gone all the way to the lake of fire fighting against God with God loving him all the way, but since he met Jesus and repented, God's love had become the path to Paul's salvation. There is not a person on planet earth that God does not love, nor is there a person who ever lived that God did not love, or stopped loving, no matter how they've lived. God loves rapists, murderers, child molesters, thieves, adulterers, fornicators, atheists, false teachers, hypocrites, liars, pornographers, child pornographers, rebellious children, dishonest politicians, Ku Klux Klansmen, Islamic extremists, gangsters, and yes, homosexuals, and anyone else who may have been left off this list. God even loved Adolf Hitler! But that love alone will not give anyone a pass into eternal life nor will it condone any one of those persons' sinful behavior. His love does, however, make it possible for any of us to be forgiven and saved, no matter how we have lived. God's love is the *path* to everlasting life, but not everlasting life itself.

The error of the religious proponents of homosexuality is that they question how that anyone can deny "love" between any two people who wish to express that "love" to each other, since God is love. But God is also *holy*. Many people do not understand God's holiness. They erroneously think God's love to be the same as their romantic or sexual inclinations and that somehow God will side with them on those bases. This reiterates what was brought out earlier in this book—that many people who call themselves Christians have no idea at all about what the bible teaches or what its overall message is. Being holy, God cannot tolerate sin at all. He cannot justify nor validate it. He cannot look upon it. He can only condemn it because it permanently stains whatever it touches. However, God sent Jesus as a propitiation,[135] that is, as a means of mercy, so that He can fully eradicate the stain of sin from believers in a way that pleases Him so that we can receive eternal life. That propitiation is the result of His love. That is why it can be said that God loves us, because in spite of His attitude towards our sin, He still made a way for us to be forgiven.

Why Some Gays Think They Can't Change

Sometimes gay people will come to church under conviction looking for a change. They will sometimes, after that experience, erroneously end up thinking that they cannot change, because their experience is that when they went to church they expected a life change, but they discover that they continued to have the same feelings and desires. They tend to believe that those feelings and desires should have completely disappeared and that they should have had no more problems with homosexual desires at all if they turned to God. Because the desires and feelings are still there, they resign themselves to those desires and feelings and then eventually come to the erroneous conclusion that perhaps God made them gay and does not want to change them, or He does not necessarily want them to change.

A Truth People Need To Understand

What is going to be presented here is a fact that many people, gay or otherwise do not understand about themselves. As a matter of fact, many Christians are not up front, or just simply quiet about a lot of things that pertain to their personal human nature. This is understandable, because if truth be told, the revelation of what some Christians may struggle with internally would be embarrassing. Sometimes, Christians struggle internally with some pretty evil things. We sometimes call that struggle *temptation*. And sometimes, others just simply give in to the desires that they are having. The news headlines are replete with some of those accounts. But through Christ and the word of God many believers do learn how to overcome temptation. Still some will have greater difficulty and their struggles will continue for a while. I learned in my early years that inner temptation and ungodly desires are themselves not sin, but <u>yielding</u> to those desires is sin. Temptation, which is based in inner desire, is something that starts in the body overwhelming the mind with desire, and is manifested in strong feelings. A person can be sorry for their sin, repent, turn to Jesus, and genuinely ask Him for forgiveness and make Him the Lord of their lives—and still experience the desires and feelings that plagued him before he came to Christ, because the body and the feelings and the desires that it has, are still there. The body is not born again, but your mind and your spirit are born again and renewed. The sinful flesh, that is the desire of the human nature, has to be "put to death" by each of us.

> *[F]or if you are living according to the flesh, you must die; but if by the Spirit you are putting to death the deeds of the body, you will live.* Rom 8:13-14 NASU

> *And they that are Christ's have crucified the flesh with the affections and lusts.* Galatians 5:24

Remember in the Torah how people were "put to death" for doing certain things? Well, the real lesson from those penalties is that God wants every one of us to put those <u>behaviors</u> to death. The law condemned the flesh in sin, but Jesus condemned sin in the flesh, so that we could satisfy the righteous demands of the law through Him.

> *For what the law could not do, in that it was weak through the flesh, God sending his own Son in the likeness of sinful flesh, and for sin, condemned sin in the flesh: That the righteousness of the law might be fulfilled in us, who walk not after the flesh, but after the Spirit.* Romans 8:3-4

An important fact that many people who first turn to God do not realize is that *desire does not have to be satisfied*. I had given a very telling personal experience in chapter 9 of some of my own immoral problems that I had experienced in my teen years before I came to Christ. After I came to Christ, what he took away was my desire to sin, not my desire to have sex. Besides, I would not have wanted Him to take that away anyway! Instead I learned how to deny the body its sinful sexual desires and instead chose to wait until marriage in accordance with God's will. Since I wanted to please God, He gave me the strength to not sinfully fulfill my sexual desires in a wanton manner at any expense. Jesus said:

> . . . *"If anyone wishes to come after Me, he must deny himself, and take up his cross and follow Me*. Mark 8:34 NASU

What God had given me was something that I had not had before—control. About a month after I got saved, I met the girl who would become my wife. During the time of our three year courtship, I was amazed at the control and strength that I suddenly had. I still strongly desired sex, but my desire to please God became greater than my desire to engage in unmarried sex. God had given me the ability to resist what I wanted in favor of what He wanted. The sexual desire was still strong—very strong—sometimes painfully strong. But God gave me the willpower to resist fulfilling it sinfully. From the day I came to Jesus Christ, I was even able to overcome the desire to masturbate. I lived completely celibate for the next three years. For me, that was a major miracle. Before that, I could not go three days without satisfying my desires in some manner.

Many people equate their feelings and desires with sin. They think that they have sinned if they have the feelings which are rooted in desire. In the case of homosexuals, when they experience sexual desire, because of years of conditioning—not genetics, their desire will be for the kind of sex and companionship that they had become accustomed to. They do not realize that if they learn to deny the body of what it wants as Jesus taught, the mind will eventually lose its will to satisfy the sin that the body wants, because God will give them the strength to resist fulfilling those sinful desires and to do what He wants. When a person is saved, his mind is renewed. Renewal results in reconditioning. Over time, denying the body of sinful desire causes the will to satisfy those sinful desires to wane. This does not mean that they will immediately have a desire for the opposite sex. They will simply lose the desire to sin against God. And any feeling or temptation that they may experience from within, they will overcome it without sin. They will refuse to satisfy it because of their overwhelming desire to please God. At the same time, the renewed mind becomes stronger and begins to take more control. The renewed mind then controls the body rather than vice-versa, and that mind will perfer to do the will of God. This is what Paul meant when he wrote,

> *[B]ut I discipline my body and make it my slave, so that, after I have preached to others, I myself will not be disqualified.* 1 Corinthians 9:26-27 NASU*

While we are in sin, the body is controlling us. We obey its impulses and do what it wants and give it what it wants. Expounding on that idea, the bible says:

> *And you He made alive, who were dead in trespasses and sins, in which you once walked according to the course of this world, according to the prince of the power of the air, the spirit who now works in the sons of disobedience, among whom also we all once conducted ourselves in the lusts of our flesh, fulfilling the desires of the flesh and of the mind, and were by nature children of wrath, just as the others.* Eph 2:1-3 NKJV

Notice that Paul says that before we became believers, we fulfilled the desires of the flesh. The Greek word for flesh is *sarx* which refers to the body as opposed to the soul. Extensively, it refers to the human nature that drives the body in action and behavior, and an earthly nature that acts on its own and either rejects or does not have any divine influence.[136] Notice the order presented: body **first**, mind **second**. Paul, writing to believers, said that all people before they became believers fulfilled the desires of the body and of the mind. In those pre-salvation days, the mind may want to do what it knows is right, and it may even want to serve God. But it can't because the body is addicted to the pleasurable sensations caused by sin and it craves them. The body desires certain things, and then the mind relents, and then justifies. Outside of any influence from God, that is the order of fleshly sins. While we are imprisoned in this condition, God means little to us where obeying Him is concerned. While we may have some respect for Him, our god is our body, and so we tend to follow its desires rather than the desires of our Creator. Paul wrote,

> *For many walk, of whom I have told you often, and now tell you even weeping, that they are the enemies of the cross of Christ: Whose end is destruction, whose God is their belly, and whose glory is in their shame, who mind earthly things.* Philippians 3:18-19

Paul, using the word *belly*, meant that their god is the body's fleshly appetites. What the body wants, the body gets! The more we follow our human desires, the more we want them and are conditioned to fulfill them. The apostle Paul wrote again,

> Who being past feeling have given them-selves over unto lasciviousness, to work all uncleanness with greediness. Eph 4:19

Homosexuals do not realize it, but they condition themselves to what they desire. This is true of all sexual immorality. Mental conditioning where sexuality is concerned can give us tunnel vision to the extent that we only want and enjoy what we have been practicing. In the process, we lose our sense of conscience, which is the meaning of the phrase "past feeling." The conscience no longer bothers us when we are completely given over to our sin. As a pastor I have counseled individuals, for example, who although they were married, could not engage sexually with their wives, but preferred to masturbate instead. Their behavior came from conditioning by habit of practice. The only way to overcome that kind of conditioning is to deny the desire to masturbate. Then, with God's help, turn that sexual attention to his wife. God will help him and eventually his mind will be retrained to enjoy the woman God has given him. There are certain types of pedophiles who cannot sustain a sexual relationship with adults because their minds have been so conditioned until their sexual partner must be below a certain age. Once that partner has reached that age limit, the pedophile's mind cannot process a normal sexual relationship with them anymore. Therefore, they must seek out a new partner who is at the younger age they prefer. That is because they have conditioned their own minds in this manner. Once called *chicken hawks,* some men prefer only boys who are 15 or younger. After the persons they are sexual with reaches the age of 15, they will revert to a younger person. Then there are people who cannot enjoy sex unless it's in a group, or unless it involves bondage or pain, or unless it involves pornography or some kind of role-playing. All of these kinds of individuals have had their minds conditioned in these ways and it has affected their sexual behavior and activity.

These things helps us to understand why God goes after your mind. The bible teaches,

And do not be conformed to this world, but be transformed by the renewing of your mind, so that you may prove what the will of God is, that which is good and acceptable and perfect. Romans 12:2 NASU

God renews our minds and it is necessary for us to allow Him to do so. In the renewing process, He reconditions our minds so that we might do His will, rather than the will of the flesh. He conditions our minds to follow the leadership of His Spirit, who gives us the strength to carry out His will. Satan on the other hand, aims at the flesh. When Satan tempted Jesus, he aimed at Jesus' human nature and tempted Him to satisfy the hunger in His body by using the power of God to serve Himself selfishly.[137] Jesus however, refused to yield to that temptation. Later on, Jesus revealed Satan's goal when Peter unwittingly followed a suggestion from Satan to contend with Him. Jesus told Satan to "get behind me" and then showed that Satan's influence was a aimed at one thing only – the desire of man.[138] While God appeals to the mind, Satan appeals to the body and to the desire to provoke greater sinful desire to get *his* will done. He makes sure that man will work hard to fulfill fleshly pleasure and desires—especially those that are contrary to God. God works to renew the mind and the desires of the mind, so that the mind's desire would be to please Him and deny the flesh. Apart from that, no man will please God.

This is the battle of every human being. In the beginning, most of us fight God tooth and nail and resist Him adamantly just as Paul did. He reaches out to us and we rebuff His attempts. He lovingly tells us that we are sinners (through others) and we angrily reject God's message through them and accuse them of wanting us to live by "their" rules. We cry about our freedoms and the constitution, not realizing that we are rejecting God and His love. Then we turn back to our evil ways that according to His law, are worthy of death. The objective of the law was always to identify sin and execute the judgement for it. But God does not immediately execute the death penalty. Instead, He gives us mercy (afforded to us by the blood of Jesus and His love), and allows us to continue doing what we have been conditioned to do, while still reaching out to us to repent. And Jesus satisfied the demand of the law by receiving the execution of the penalty of sin for us.

We are not saved by doing the works of the law, but we are saved by the blood of Jesus Christ. Then, we strive to live in obedience to His word as taught to us by Jesus and His apostles. We live in obedience to Him because we love Him and not because we are trying to earn salvation or His attention. When Jesus forgives and saves us, we are given salvation and eternal life at that very moment. So there is nothing you have to do to earn salvation. Living in obedience is not earning salvation, but it is living in love. Jesus said:

> *If ye love me, keep my commandments. John 14:15*

and,

> *. . . If a man love me, he will keep my words: and my Father will love him, and we will come unto him, and make our abode with him. John 14:23*

Paul added:

> *Owe no man any thing, but to love one another: for he that loveth another hath fulfilled the law. For this, Thou shalt not commit adultery, Thou shalt not kill, Thou shalt not steal, Thou shalt not bear false witness, Thou shalt not covet; and if there be any other commandment, it is briefly comprehended in this saying, namely, Thou shalt love thy neighbour as thyself. Love worketh no ill to his neighbour: therefore love is the fulfilling of the law. Rom 13:8-10*

Did you catch that? All of the commandments are rooted in love. If I love you, I won't steal from you. I will treat you as I want you to treat me,[139] and I will treat you as I would treat myself.[140] If I love God, then I will do what He wants. When we discussed the forced sex laws earlier, that was only the consequential portion that dealt with the violators. But the purpose of the Torah is to produce love. If a young man taught in the law of God would abide by that law, he would not violate a young woman in the first place seeing the precarious position it could put her in. If he genuinely loved her, he would not work any "ill" towards her, thus fulfilling an objective of the Torah. But since there is a man bent on living by his own desire in violation of the Torah, then the Torah would *force* him to care for (love) the woman he violated for the rest of his life, and conversely, force the female who was violated to forgive him! To understand the value of that forced love and forgiveness, one must ask if eternal life is worth that. Also, pay close attention to what Jesus taught:

> *"For if you forgive others for their transgressions, your heavenly Father will also forgive you. "But if you do not forgive others, then your Father will not forgive your transgressions.* Matt 6:14-16 NASU

Nonetheless, all women and girls would be safe in the presence of those who obediently followed the Torah's law of love.

Loving God With All the Heart

If God is my first love, then anything that He wants me to do, or not do, I will comply. My love for God must be more important than anything else, otherwise, I have another god and am committing idolatry. When I love Him, then I want His will over and above my own. And His will, of course, is that I love my neighbor and work no ill will towards him or her, even if he or she is not obeying God in certain matters, and even if they choose to be my enemies![141] Therein is the truth about love.

Before we ever come to understand any of these things, we live in constant sin, and God hates sin. Yet, God does not bring immediate judgment upon us that we rightfully deserve according to the law because of His loving patience. Peter wrote:

> *The Lord is . . . patient toward you, not wishing for any to perish but for all to come to repentance.* 2 Peter 3:9 NASU

Peter certainly understood patience. He lied and denied the Lord.[142] He allowed Satan to influence him and disrespect his Master.[143] He along with the other disciples forsook Jesus and fled when He was falsely arrested.[144] Despite all of his faults, Jesus was eager to love him, be with him, and use him to encourage the other apostles even before his denial.[145] But Jesus patiently waited for him to mature.

God is patient towards us and allows us to continue to do our evil deeds waiting for us to get tired, or for our behaviors to get us into a bind, and cause us to run to Him. He does not care how or when we come to Him (sooner is better), and He will not hold it against us if we come running later after we are all messed up by our lifestyles because He really loves us.

If any of you reading this chapter recognize yourselves and realize God's love for you, you can

come to Him right now and He will accept you—
no matter what you've done—even if everyone else
rejects you. If you are having problem with any evil
lifestyle, whether sex, drugs, dishonesty, or anything else, all you need to do is come repenting to
Jesus, acknowledging that you are a helpless sinner
who deserves any judgment God would bring upon
you and fall on His mercy and forgiveness and He
will receive and forgive you. That is what God's
love is really all about. Also, confess to Him what
your weaknesses are and ask Him to help you to
deny your flesh and then turn your whole life over
to Him. He will help you by rebirthing your spirit
and renewing your mind. He will also help you
to recondition your mind by a new life practice in
His word and His Spirit. His love will carry you
all the way from weakness to strength. You come
to God by coming to Jesus and receiving forgiveness through His blood which was shed for your
redemption and deliverance for sin. When you turn
to Christ, He accepts you, no matter how badly your
life is messed up and tangled up. He knows how to
straighten out the mess. You must simply come to
Him just like you are and acknowledge (confess)
that your life is a mess and that you are turning it
over to Him for Him to straighten out. He knows
how to do that better than you do. If you could have
straightened out your messy life, you would have
done it already. But being in sin is like being mired
and sinking into a deep mud pit. You cannot get out
by yourself. David said:

He lifted me out of the pit of despair,
out of the mud and the mire.
He set my feet on solid ground
and steadied me as I walked along.
Ps 40:2 NLT

Now after He pulls you out, then, you must find a good bible believing, Jesus loving, and people loving church that teaches holy living and righteousness, but yet understands mercy and grace. (Believe me, those can be very hard to find), but that is what will help you to overcome anything that would otherwise hinder you from pleasing God, learning about Him, and receiving eternal life.

The flip side of everlasting life is eternal damnation. The bible teaches:

But the fearful, and unbelieving, and the abominable, and murderers, and whoremongers, and sorcerers, and idolaters, and all liars, shall have their part in the lake which burneth with fire and brimstone: which is the second death. Revelation 21:8

Everyone who is lost and outside of the salvation of Jesus Christ will burn forever in the lake of fire. This book instructs on how to avoid such horrendous eternal punishment.

One might ask, "How can a loving God exact that kind of punishment?" The reason is due to His holiness. But His mercy allows us to live on, and even continue in sin, allowing us time to repent. If we don't, it's our fault, not His. His holiness will demand righteous justice according to the Torah which is eternal punishment. Jesus died in our place for that reason so that we, although we do not deserve it, can inherit everlasting life rather than receive everlasting damnation. I have just described *salvation* which is given to us as a gift by the love of God.

Chapter Twelve

Final Words

*T*hese are the days of the son of man, meaning that we are living in the days that preceed the return of Jesus to the earth. He taught that there would be many signs experienced in the earth that would be seen just before He returned. One of those signs is:

> *Likewise also as it was in the days of Lot;*
> *they did eat, they drank, they bought, they*
> *sold, they planted, they builded;*
> *But the same day that Lot went out of Sodom*
> *it rained fire and brimstone from heaven, and*
> *destroyed them all.*
> *Even thus shall it be in the day when the Son*
> *of man is revealed. Luke 17:28-30*

In the early to mid 1970s, I was a young minister in my 20s. I recall the Holy Spirit revealing to me the full extent of what that scripture meant. At that time, open homosexuality was still considered shameful and most homosexuals were still hiding their lifestyles "in the closet." They had just begun to revolt against the norm of the label of immorality, a characteristic which is labeled by God and not by man. The Holy Spirit revealed to me that a time would come when homosexuality would no longer be considered shameful in the world thus causing it to become like Sodom in incessant immorality before Jesus returned. At the time, parents also were more acutely aware of what their children did and tried hard to promote moral decency where sexuality was concerned. The Lord also showed me that the time would come when many parents would be more accepting of their children having sex right in the home and they would know it, but not be concerned or alarmed, and even encourage it. Because of the over-sexualization of our society, these things are happening right now, demonstrating that the coming of Jesus Christ is dangerously (for many) near. What we must really be aware and concerned about is that the worst is yet to come. Because of sin and the rejection of God's standards, the world will face the worst trouble that it has ever faced in its history. Jesus said that there would be an intense time of unprecedented tribulation on the planet that will never be repeated again.[146] But, these prevalent immoral behaviors are all signs that point to the return of Jesus Christ. The main warning that I am presenting to all who read this book is that the time to repent and do the will of God is now.

> *Know ye not that the unrighteous shall not*
> *inherit the kingdom of God? Be not deceived:*
> *neither fornicators, nor idolaters, nor*
> *adulterers, nor effeminate, nor abusers of*
> *themselves with mankind, Nor thieves, nor*
> *covetous, nor drunkards, nor revilers, nor*
> *extortioners, shall inherit the kingdom of*
> *God.* 1 Corinthians 6:9-10

Last Days

One thing that the proponents of homosexuality do not realize is the influence of demonic spirits against godly doctrine. For some, this next scripture passage will be one that is completely unknown. The Apostle Paul prophesied,

> *But the Spirit explicitly says that in later times*
> *some will fall away from the faith, paying*
> *attention to deceitful spirits and doctrines of*
> *demons . . .* 1 Tim 4:1 NASU

Paul wrote that The Holy Spirit revealed that one of the major problems of the last days, that is, the days before the return of Christ, is the infiltration of doctrines contrived by demons into the church, and people listening to them and believing them. The Apostle Peter confirmed the same by this prophecy:

> *But false prophets also arose among the*
> *people, just as there will also be false*

*teachers among you, who will secretly intro-
duce destructive heresies, even denying the
Master who bought them, bringing swift
destruction upon themselves. 2 Many will
follow their sensuality, and because of
them the way of the truth will be maligned;*
2 Peter 2:1-2 NASU

The strong language from Peter says that just
as there were false prophets in Israel in the past,
there will also be false teachers in the last days who
would spring up and introduce destructive teachings
into the church. He goes on to say that many people
will follow their unrestrained, unchaste, lewd, and
immoral teachings (the meaning of sensuality), and
speak evil of (malign) the path of the truth. For centu-
ries, Christians have understood that homosexuality
is sin. But now, true believers are accused of hatred
and being unloving and unChristianlike for sticking
with that truth, thus confirming the prophecy that
Peter gave as correct. So in these last days, Satanic
doctrine has infiltrated the church with a lie that
homosexuality is okay and many are being seduced
into believing that lie.

Then Paul adds another prophecy that anyone
who really wants to please God should take seri-
ously. He writes:

*For the time will come when they will not
endure sound doctrine; but after their own
lusts shall they heap to themselves teachers,
having itching ears;*

And they shall turn away their ears from the truth, and shall be turned unto fables.
2 Tim 4:3-4

Apparently that time has come. People nowadays look for bible teachers who will only teach what appeals to their own desires and are not interested in truthful doctrine. They would rather listen to a lie because that is what they want to believe and it sounds good to their ears. But no matter how people turn from and forsake the truth, God is not going to change His standards for you, me, or anyone else. No man can alter His standards. Like Jesus said in Luke 13:5, If we do not repent, and persist in living in sin, we will perish like anyone else. But if we obey Him, we will receive eternal life, and that is God's goal for all of us.

"He who believes in the Son has eternal life; but he who does not obey the Son will not see life, but the wrath of God abides on him."
John 3:36 NASU

REFERENCES

[1] Genesis 3:1-5
[2] Genesis 3:5-6
[3] John 8:44
[4] Genesis 3:6
[5] Genesis 3:7
[6] Genesis 3:19
[7] Galatians 3:21-22
[8] Hebrews 9:22
[9] Leviticus 16
[10] Hebrews 10:3-4
[11] Genesis 3:7,11
[12] Leviticus 15:19-24
[13] Matthew 15:2
[14] Mark 7:10-13
[15] Matthew 15:3 NASU
[16] Exodus 23:17
[17] Hebrew 9:24
[18] Romans 8:3-4
[19] Matthew 13:36; 15:15
[20] Acts 17:10-11

[21] Genesis 2:23-24
[22] Tennessee v. John Scopes, 1925
[23] Genesis 20:2
[24] Genesis 20:12

[25] Genesis 16:1-4

[26] Genesis 21:18

[27] Genesis 17:5

[28] "Sons of God" from The New Unger's Bible Dictionary. Originally published by Moody Press of Chicago, Illinois. Copyright (c) 1988.

[29] "Sons of God" from McClintock and Strong Encyclopedia, Electronic Database. Copyright © 2000, 2003 by Biblesoft, Inc.

[30] Hebrews 1:13-14

[31] Jude 6

[32] "Levirate Law" from Easton's Bible Dictionary, PC Study Bible formatted electronic database Copyright © 2003 Biblesoft, Inc.

[33] Genesis 38:18 from Layard's 'Nineveh and Babylon,' p. 608, note. Jamieson, Fausset, and Brown Commentary, Electronic Database. Copyright (c) 1997 by Biblesoft

[34] Genesis 38:29-30; 46:12

[35] Leviticus 19:9-10

[36] Ruth 4:1-5

[37] 1 Samuel 13:14

[38] 1 Samuel 17:25; 18:19

[39] 1 Samuel 18:27

[40] 2 Samuel 6:23

[41] 2 Samuel 11:15

[42] 2 Samuel 11:27; 12:13

[43] 1 Kings 11:3

[44] Deuteronomy 17:17; 1 Kings 11:1-2

[45] 1 Kings 11:2

[46] Ecclesiastes 2:8

[47] 1 Kings 11:5-10

[48] Matthew 23:11;

[49] Ephesians 5:22; 1 Peter 5:5-6

[50] "KJV: Harlot: Strong's number OT:2181in Genesis 38:15" from Vine's Expository Dictionary of Biblical Words, Copyright © 1985, Thomas Nelson Publishers

[51] Derteronomy 22:13-14 from Keil & Delitzsch Commentary on the Old Testament: New Updated Edition, Electronic Database. Copyright (c) 1996 by Hendrickson Publishers, Inc.

[52] Deuteronomy 22:15 from Adam Clarke's Commentary, Electronic Database. Copyright (c) 1996 by Biblesoft)

[53] Isaiah 54:5

[54] Matthew 1:18-20

[55] "Matthew 1:18" from Adam Clarke's Commentary, Electronic Database. Copyright (c) 1996 by Biblesoft

[56] Leviticus 20:14

[57] Exodus 24:18

[58] Matthew 7:1-2

[59] Exodus 5:6-14

[60] Exodus 3:1-8,19; 4:21

[61] Exodus 3:20

[62] Exodus 6:7

[63] Exodus 12:29

[64] Exodus 14:26-28

[65] Exodus 3:1-6

[66] Malachi 2:16

[67] Exodus 21:7-10

[68] "Concubine" from Easton's Bible Dictionary, PC Study Bible formatted electronic database Copyright © 2003 Biblesoft, Inc. All rights reserved.)

[69] Judges 14:3: Genesis 29:18

[70] "dowry" from The New Unger's Bible Dictionary. Originally published by Moody Press of Chicago, Illinois. Copyright (c) 1988.)

[71] "Genesis 34:1-2" from Keil & Delitzsch Commentary on the Old Testament: New Updated Edition, Electronic Database. Copyright (c) 1996 by Hendrickson Publishers, Inc.

[72] Genesis 34:30-31

[73] Proverbs 29:18

[74] Deuteronomy 29:23

[75] Genesis 19:21-23,30

[76] Helminiak, Daniel A. (2000) The Abomination of Leviticus: Uncleanness. What the Bible *Really* Says About Homosexuality (p. 51). Tajique, NM: Alamo Square Press

[77] Boswell, John. (1980). The Scriptures. Christianity, Social Tolerance, and Homosexuality. (p. 101-102). Chicago, IL: University of Chicago Press.

[78] Boswell, John. (1980). The Scriptures. Christianity, Social Tolerance, and Homosexuality. (p. 100). Chicago, IL: University of Chicago Press.

[79] Boswell, John. (1980). The Scriptures. Christianity, Social Tolerance, and Homosexuality. (p. 100). Chicago, IL: University of Chicago Press.

[80] Leviticus 18:27

[81] Judges 2:16

[82] "Judge" from LEVERTOFF, PAUL; B.D., Professor of Old and Talmudic Literature at Institutum Delitzschianum at Leipzig, Germany. Articles: First-Fruits, Judge, Oath, Proselyte Sanhedrin, Synagogue, Tithe, Vow, Witness.
(from International Standard Bible Encyclopaedia, Electronic Database Copyright (c)1996 by Biblesoft)

[83] Judges 17:6

[84] "Deuteronomy 23:17" from Keil & Delitzsch Commentary on the Old Testament: New Updated Edition, Electronic Database. Copyright (c) 1996 by Hendrickson Publishers, Inc.)

[85] "KJV: effeminate: 79.100: Strong's number NT:3120 from Greek-English Lexicon Based on Semantic Domain. Copyright (c) 1988 United Bible Societies, New York. Used by permission.

[86] Retrieved, September 15, 2005 from www.pantheon.org/areas/gallery/mythology/europe/greek/ganymede.html

[87] "KJV: effeminate: 88:281: Strong's number NT:3120 from Greek-English Lexicon Based on Semantic Domain. Copyright (c) 1988 United Bible Societies, New York. Used by permission.

[88] NT:733 (Biblesoft's New Exhaustive Strong's Numbers and Concordance with Expanded Greek-Hebrew Dictionary.

Copyright © 1994, 2003 Biblesoft, Inc. and International Bible Translators, Inc.)

[89] "KJV: Abusers of themselves with mankind: 88:280: Strong's number NT:733 from Greek-English Lexicon Based on Semantic Domain. Copyright (c) 1988 United Bible Societies, New York. Used by permission.

[90] NT:1608 (from Thayer's Greek Lexicon, Electronic Database. Copyright (c) 2000 by Biblesoft)1608 from NT:1537 and NT:4203; (Biblesoft's New Exhaustive Strong's Numbers and Concordance with Expanded Greek-Hebrew Dictionary. Copyright © 1994, 2003 Biblesoft, Inc. and International Bible Translators, Inc.)

[91] Acts 9:1-2

[92] Acts 9:4-5

[93] Mark 11:27-33

[94] 1 Peter 1:9-12

[95] Genesis 1:28

[96] Genesis 6:3

[97] John 3:16-19

[98] 2 Timothy 3:16

[99] Boswell, John. (1980). The Scriptures. Christianity, Social Tolerance, and Homosexuality. (p. 109). Chicago, IL: University of Chicago Press.

[100] Rom 1:26 (from Interlinear Transliterated Bible. Copyright © 1994, 2003 by Biblesoft, Inc.)

[101] 1 John 4:8,16

[102] Helminiak, Daniel A. (2000) Purity Concerns in the Christian Testament. What the Bible *Really* Says About Homosexuality (p. 73). Tajique, NM: Alamo Square Press.

[103] Helminiak, Daniel A. (2000) Interpreting the Bible. What the Bible *Really* Says About Homosexuality (p. 39). Tajique, NM: Alamo Square Press.

[104] Luke 17:26

[105] 2 Timothy 4:3; 1 Timothy 4:1

[106] John 8:32

[107] Helminiak, Daniel A. (2000) Purity Concerns in the Christian Testament. What the Bible *Really* Says About Homosexuality (p. 70). Tajique, NM: Alamo Square Press.

[108] Helminiak, Daniel A. (2000 Purity Concerns in the Christian Testament. What the Bible *Really* Says About Homosexuality (p. 70). Tajique, NM: Alamo Square Press.

[109] Helminiak, Daniel A. (2000) Interpreting the Bible. The Sin of Sodom: Inhospitality. What the Bible *Really* Says About Homosexuality (p. 46-47). Tajique, NM: Alamo Square Press.

[110] Boswell, John. (1980). The Scriptures. Christianity, Social Tolerance, and Homosexuality. (p. 93). Chicago, IL: University of Chicago Press.

[111] Boswell, John. (1980). The Scriptures. Christianity, Social Tolerance, and Homosexuality. (p. 94). Chicago, IL: University of Chicago Press.

[112] Helminiak, Daniel A. (2000) The Sin of Sodom: Inhospitality. What the Bible *Really* Says About Homosexuality (p. 48). Tajique, NM: Alamo Square Press.

[113] Helminiak, Daniel A. (2000) The Sin of Sodom: Inhospitality. What the Bible *Really* Says About Homosexuality (p. 44). Tajique, NM: Alamo Square Press.

[114] Helminiak, Daniel A. (2000) The Sin of Sodom: Inhospitality. What the Bible *Really* Says About Homosexuality (p. 45). Tajique, NM: Alamo Square Press.

[115] Boswell, John. (1980). The Scriptures. Christianity, Social Tolerance, and Homosexuality. (p. 94). Chicago, IL: University of Chicago Press.

116 *Know*: Genesis 19:5; Judges 19:22; Luke 1:34; *Knew*: Genesis 4:1,17,25; 38:26; Judges 11:39; 19:25; 1Samuel 1:19; 1Kings 1:4; Matthew 1:25: *Known*: Genesis 19:8; 24:16; Numbers 31:17,18,35; Judges 21:12

117 1 Samuel 18:4

118 1 Sam 20:33

119 1 Samuel 31:1-2

120 2 Samuel 1:26

121 1 Samuel 18:18

122 1 Samuel 18:19-27

123 Ruth 1:11

124 Helminiak, Daniel A. (2000) Other Supposed References to Homosexuality. What the Bible *Really* Says About Homosexuality (p. 126). Tajique, NM: Alamo Square Press.

125 Helminiak, Daniel A. (2000) Other Supposed References to Homosexuality. What the Bible *Really* Says About Homosexuality (p. 127). Tajique, NM: Alamo Square Press.

126 "KJV: tender love: TWOT number 2146a: Strong's number 7356" Theological Wordbook of the Old Testament. Copyright (c) 1980 by The Moody Bible Institute of Chicago. All rights reserved. Used by permission.

127 Daniel 1:3-4

128 1 Corinthians 6:18

129 Myerson, Alan (Director). 1981. *Private Lessons* [Motion picture]. United States. Copyright© The Z Review

130 Cuesta, Michael (Director). 2001. *L.I.E.* [Motion picture].

131 Bergendahl, Waldemar (Producer). Hallström, Lasse (Director). 1985. *My Live as a Dog* [Motion picture]. Canada

132 Retrieved July 6, 2012 from http://www.radaronline.com/exclusives/2011/08/thylane-loubry-blondeau-child-model-french-vogue-kiddie-porn-video

133 Retrieved April 23, 2004 from http://www.foxnews.com/story/0,2933,117822,00.html

134 Romans 3:10

135 1 John 2:2; 1 John 4:10; Romans 3:25; Hebrews 2:17

[136] "KJV-flesh: NT:4561" (from Thayer's Greek Lexicon, Electronic Database. Copyright © 2000, 2003 by Biblesoft, Inc. All rights reserved.
[137] Matthew 4:3
[138] Matthew 16:23
[139] Luke 6:31
[140] Mark 12:31
[141] Luke 6:27
[142] Matthew 26:69-75
[143] Matthew 16:22
[144] Mark 14:50,53
[145] Luke 22:32-34
[146] Matthew 24:21

Milton Keynes UK
Ingram Content Group UK Ltd.
UKHW012129110624
443988UK00001B/25